EDITING POETRY FROM SPENSER TO DRYDEN

Conference on Editorial Problems

Previous Conference Publications

1965 *Editing Sixteenth-Century Texts*, ed. R. J. Schoeck (1966)

1966 *Editing Nineteenth-Century Texts*, ed. John M. Robson (1967)

1967 *Editing Eighteenth-Century Texts*, ed. D. I. B. Smith (1968)

1968 *Editor, Author and Publisher*, ed. William J. Howard (1969)

1969 *Editing Twentieth-Century Texts*, ed. Francess G. Halpenny (1972)

1970 *Editing Seventeenth-Century Prose*, ed. D. I. B. Smith (1972)

1971 *Editing Texts of the Romantic Period*, ed. John D. Baird (1972)

1972 *Editing Canadian Texts*, ed. Francess G. Halpenny (1975)

1973 *Editing Eighteenth-Century Novels*, ed. G. E. Bentley, Jr. (1975)

1974 *Editing British and American Literature, 1880–1920*, ed. Eric W. Domville (1976)

1975 *Editing Renaissance Dramatic Texts: English, Italian, and Spanish*, ed. Anne Lancashire (1976)

1976 *Editing Medieval Texts: English, French, and Latin Written in England*, ed. A. G. Rigg (1977)

1977 *Editing Nineteenth-Century Fiction*, ed. Jane Millgate (1978)

1978 *Editing Correspondence*, ed. J. A. Dainard (1979)

1979 *Editing Illustrated Books*, ed. William Blissett (1980)

The Conference volume for 1981 will deal with the editing of texts in the history of science and medicine and will be edited by Trevor H. Levere.

Copies of all previous volumes are available through
Garland Publishing Inc.

EDITING POETRY FROM SPENSER TO DRYDEN

Papers given at the sixteenth annual
Conference on Editorial Problems,
University of Toronto,
31 October–1 November 1980

EDITED BY A.H. DE QUEHEN

Garland Publishing, Inc., New York & London

1981

Library of Congress Cataloging in Publication Data

Conference on Editorial Problems (16th : 1980 : University of Toronto)
Editing poetry from Spenser to Dryden.

Includes index.
Contents: Introduction / A.H. de Quehen — Problems in editing Donne's Songs and sonets / Mark Roberts — Editing from manuscript: Cowley and the Cowper papers / Allan Pritchard — [etc.]
1. English poetry—Early modern, 1500–1700—Criticism, Textual—Congresses. 2. Editing—Congresses. I. Quehen, A.H. de. II. Title.
PR543.C6 1980 801'.951 81-47627
ISBN 0-8240-2431-1 AACR2

Printed on acid-free, 250-year-life paper
Manufactured in the United States of America

Contents

List of Illustrations

Cowley's *The Civil War* in Panshanger MS. D/EP/F48, plates 1 and 2, and in Panshanger MS. D/EP/F36, plate 3. Reproduced by permission of Lady Ravensdale and the Hertfordshire County Record Office.

Dryden's *Works of Virgil* (1697). Reproduced by permission of the Thomas Fisher Rare Book Library, University of Toronto.

Notes on Contributors

WILLIAM FROST is Professor of English in the University of California, Santa Barbara. His Dryden studies include *Dryden and the Art of Translation* and extensive editorial work, most recently in the California Dryden's *Poems 1693–1696* (Vol. IV) and *Poems 1697* (the Virgil translation, forthcoming as Vols. V and VI). He was also associate editor of *Pope's Iliad and Odyssey* in the Twickenham edition.

A. C. HAMILTON is Professor of English in Queen's University, Kingston. He is author of *The Structure of Allegory in "The Faerie Queene"*, *The Early Shakespeare*, and *Sir Philip Sidney: A Study of His Life and Works.* He is editor of *The Faerie Queene* in Longmans Annotated English Poets.

R. G. MOYLES is Professor of English in the University of Alberta, Edmonton. He is author of *English-Canadian Literature to 1900* and of bibliographical articles on Milton. He is currently completing a study of the textual history of *Paradise Lost.*

ALLAN PRITCHARD is Professor of English in the University of Toronto, appointed to University College. He is editor of Cowley's *The Civil War* and author of articles on George Wither, Anthony Wood, and other seventeenth-century subjects. His most recent work has centred on the Wood manuscripts in the Bodleian Library.

MARK ROBERTS is Professor of English in the University of Keele. He is author of *Browning's Men and Women*, *The Tradition of Romantic Morality*, and *The Fundmentals of Literary Criticism.* He is preparing a critical edition of the poems of John Donne for Longmans Annotated English Poets.

EDITING POETRY FROM SPENSER TO DRYDEN

Introduction

A.H. de Quehen

In 1970 the Sixth Conference on Editorial Problems was devoted to Editing Seventeenth-Century Prose, and ten years later the Sixteenth Conference has returned to that demanding period and its poetry. The Conference was held at the University of Toronto on 31 October and 1 November 1980, with the customary five papers being presented. They comment on all stages of an editor's progress, from manuscript archives to annotation of the established text, and consider a wide range of poetic genres from lyric to epic translation. The earliest examples are drawn from Spenser, and the latest poet discussed is Dryden; hence comes the title of the Conference and this volume.

In his paper on Donne's text, Mark Roberts's central theme is the broad issue of "principle" versus "taste". It is arguable whether an editor should be subject to the dictates of principle – but not unless a comprehensive principle can first be formulated. There is no hope of such a principle in the *Songs and Sonets.* Given the contamination between manuscripts even of different traditions, the progress of error is traceable only in some fairly simple instances. In more complex cases, hypotheses are dubious if only because they tend to conflict in their general implications. Yet even when each problem must be dealt with on its own terms, those terms must conform to a working theory of the text that will express the characteristics of the manuscript groups and suggest, in the choice of readings, certain probabilities or limitations to be taken into account. In his analysis of three poems – "A Valediction forbidding Mourning", "The Flea", and "The Good-Morrow" – Professor Roberts shows how very full the complete account must be, especially in judging whether variant readings may derive from different authorial versions. Much depends on the reader's confidence in the editor's judgement, and in the study of Donne that command of the field which Professor Roberts praises in Grierson is hard won over many years. From his analysis of the newly discovered Dalhousie manuscript to his argument for eclecticism in "The Good-Morrow" Professor Roberts shows the greatest skill over a course where clear rounds are rare indeed.

The manuscript miscellanies of the seventeenth century have a special fascination. They reveal individual taste as a published collection can hardly do, and through their folios one can share the private pleasures of poetry-readers of another age. But curiosity about those readers must in most cases remain unsatisfied; the manuscripts have become anonymous, long dispersed from the libraries in which they first held a favoured place. The Cowper Papers are a splendid example of an archive that has survived intact, unexplored until Allan Pritchard's interest in Cowley led to his discovery of first one, and then a second, manuscript of *The Civil War,* previously known only in the first of the three books Cowley wrote. The miscellanist herself, Sarah Cowper, left an interesting diary that throws light both on her choice of poems and on their provenance. Her collection included unpublished poems by Rochester, Buckingham, and Sedley (two of the Sedley attributions being hitherto unknown). Professor Pritchard worked first on a much corrupted version of *The Civil War,* and his subsequent discovery of the superior manuscript enabled him to check the success of his reconstruction. The conclusions he draws are cautionary, and he points to the obscurities that still remain to plague the annotator of a political poem. Lastly, he turns to another archive, of related interest: the Evelyn manuscripts and two unpublished poems which Evelyn wrote to Cowley. The second, an elegy and tribute to their long friendship, is quoted in its entirety.

While papers at these conferences have often begun with some account of an author's early editors, Gordon Moyles's paper is the first devoted exclusively to textual history. *Paradise Lost* is well suited to this approach, since the text had been seriously corrupted by the early 1730's, and was then progressively restored through the twenty years following. The catalyst of change was Bentley's edition of 1732: in reaction, offended readers looked back to the first editions. Bentley's marginal conjectures have remained notorious; but his eminence as a classicist has fostered the belief that his text itself must have been based on careful scrutiny and collation of authoritative editions. Professor Moyles shows that nothing could be further from the truth. Bentley's handling of the text was extremely casual, marked by simple failure to distinguish authoritative editions from others. It was also dishonest, for Bentley's hypothesis of a "phantom editor" obliged him to conceal the existence of the Book I manuscript, which he had manifestly used. Professor Moyles describes the three phases of the reaction to Bentley: first the banter of the wits, then collection by scholars of textual materials, and finally Newton's production of his variorum edition, the first definitive text.

The text of Dryden was never so abused; but its annotation is always demanding. The great Virgil translation presents many problems despite, and in part because of, the attention given over the centuries to the Latin original. For a start, Dryden's editor must distinguish contemporary references, not only in the translated text, but in the *Aeneis* Dedication and even in the plates and the choice of their dedicatees. Then there is Dryden's use of other Latin editions to supplement his primary text, that of Ruaeus; and, most difficult of all, the relation of Dryden's translation to the work of some fifty others who had rendered at least some part of Virgil into English (not to mention de Segrais and other European translators). From William Frost's account one readily imagines how hard it is to determine whether Dryden derived a particular nuance from a particular source and what significance these borrowings may have for the meaning of the poem. In conclusion, Professor Frost observes that Virgil's translators were a remarkably independent-minded group of men. Their lives suggest something of what they saw in Virgil, and it was surely not the unimaginative time-server imagined by Robert Graves.

A. C. Hamilton develops a theory of annotation. He begins where in English works this art itself began, with E. K.'s gloss on Spenser's *Shepheardes Calender,* and takes other examples from Campion, Jonson, Donne, Shakespeare, Milton, and Sidney. E. K. feared that, without his annotation, "many excellent & proper deuises both in wordes and matter would passe in the speedy course of reading, either as unknowen, or as not marked"; evidently he regarded, annotation as a barrier, not an aid, to rapid reading. Hence the failure of commentators lies less in their neglect of some obscurities – Professor Hamilton opens with a splendid instance of that – than in their indifference to contextually crucial words that may be (in dictionary senses) quite simple. In showing how annotation relates to the act of reading, this last paper is reminiscent of the first; for both insist on full and mature consideration of every point. There are arbitrary principles of annotation analogous to those of textual criticism – gloss all words or senses not found in the *Concise Oxford Dictionary* – and just as likely to damage the poem's meaning. It is easy to respond that editors must be sensitive critics; but taste and scholarly principle are not in automatic agreement. Bentley's false confidence in the meaning of *Paradise Lost* remains a warning to the unprincipled interpreter, and the uninformed response of the most gifted reader is rarely an adequate substitute for the poet's own meaning: the meaning which diligent research, exemplified in these papers, will always strive to recover.

The Committee of the Conference on Editorial Problems extends its thanks to the Social Sciences and Humanities Research Council of Canada for its generous support, and to the University of Toronto for sponsoring the Conference. Thanks for financial aid go also to University College, to the Department of English, and to the Office of the Dean of the Faculty of Arts and Science. As convener of the Sixteenth Conference, I should like to express my personal thanks to the other members of the Conference Committee, especially to G. E. Bentley, Jr., Alan Dainard, Richard Landon, and Desmond Neill, to whose turns especially demanding duties fell; to William Blissett, Roman Dubinski, John Peter, Claud Thompson, and James Woodruff for their expert chairmanship of the Conference sessions; to Denton Fox for his engaging speech of welcome; and to Arlene Gold for setting the text, and to Heather Phillips and Anne Quick for the proofreading of this volume.

Problems in Editing Donne's *Songs and Sonets*

Mark Roberts

To be invited to speak about editing Donne's poetry to an audience as expert as this is a great, yet daunting honour. The problems that face an editor of Donne are difficult and varied, and the pitfalls many, though I take some comfort from the fact that this conference, by its title, proclaims itself concerned with editorial problems rather than editorial solutions. I think I know a good deal about the former; of my knowledge of the latter I am much less confident.

But of course the work of several great scholars during the present century has added vastly to our knowledge and understanding of Donne's work. The labours of Grierson, naturally, stand out. I sometimes wonder whether anyone who has not made the attempt to follow in his foosteps can fully appreciate the magnitude of his achievement in his great edition of 1912. In the days before microfilm and photostat became the normal tools of an editor's work, he collated with impressive accuracy the great majority of the most important manuscripts, he perceived and described the groups into which they fall, and by the application of sound judgement produced a text that even today requires remarkably little emendation. In addition to all this, as everyone knows, he provided explanations of a huge number of obscure points in the text, the meaning of which had largely escaped earlier generations of readers.

It is by such standards that an editor today knows his own work will be judged, and any but the supremely self-confident will at times doubt his ability to meet the standards set. Now, however, we need to try to go beyond Grierson – as several more recent editors have done – for two principal reasons, one internal, so to speak, and the other external. The external reason is the discovery of important manuscripts of which Grierson was unaware; the internal reason is Grierson's adoption of an editorial approach which nowadays look insecure.

There are only two of the new manuscripts that I want to speak about here. The first is *DC* – the Dolau Cothi manuscript in the National Library of Wales. It has been classified by Gardner as a Group II manuscript (Group II is the group on which the compiler of the copy for the first edition chiefly relied when he needed to supplement or emend his basic Group I text). But this classification of *DC* is too simple. In a number of the Songs and Sonets – often, as we shall see, those in which the variants are most important – *DC* has a pure Group I text untainted by any of the characteristic readings of Group II.[1] In others it is eclectic: indeed in several poems it is almost as if its compiler had had manuscripts of the three main groups before him and was conflating the readings from them that most suited his own taste and understanding.[2] This manuscript in fact shows considerable independence of mind, something that is not common in manuscripts as good as this. At the same time, it can certainly make silly mistakes: an amusing one occurs at lines 33–4 of the "Valediction forbidding Mourning" where DC reads:

> Such wilt thou bee to mee, who must
> Like the other Foole, obliquely rūne ...

But in general, DC offers us a good text in a hand of exemplary clarity, which again and again provides the right reading in passages where the manuscripts are divided in their testimony. In this it is somewhat like the edition of 1633: I should not care to base a text on it in preference to *1633*, but both manuscript and edition contrive, whilst standing above the battle of the groups and adopting a somewhat eclectic approach, to surprise one with the accuracy and judgement they reflect in their compilers.

The second manuscript I want to speak briefly about I shall call *Dal(1)*. This is a manuscript belonging to the Dalhousie collection, which was deposited in the Scottish Record Office by its owner, the Earl of Dalhousie, by whose kind permission I am able to say something about it here. The manuscript (GD 45/26/95/1 in the Record Office's classification) was recently discovered by Dr. Peter Beal in the course of his work for the *Index of English Literary Manuscripts*. It contains some 40 poems by Donne (Songs and Sonets, Elegies, Satires, and Verse Letters, but none of the Divine Poems), which makes it one of the smaller collections, but I regard it as of very great interest and importance because of its close relationship with *L74*, that is, Lansdowne MS. 740 in the British Library. It gives what is broadly a Group II text of the poems it contains, a text which shows a very high proportion of the variants characteristic of *L74*. With certain provisos, it can also be said that it gives the text of the poems in essentially the same order as *L74*: the situation can best be described by saying that it is *as if* the copyist of *Dal(1)* had taken "The Anagram" ("Marrye: and love thy Flavia for she") and "The

Curse" from the *L74* collection and then, becoming fascinated with Donne's poetry, had gone back to the beginning of *L74* and followed the poems in it through in sequence, copying, however, only those poems that attracted him. In other words, virtually all the poems in *Dal(1)* occur in the same order as in *L74*, but many of the poems in the sequence in *L74* are not reproduced in *Dal(1)*. The last poem by Donne in *Dal(1)* appears in *L74* at fol. 125r. There is no such obvious correspondence between the order of poems in *Dal(1)* and the standard order of the Group II manuscripts, to which, textually, both *L74* and *Dal(1)* are related.

Dal(1), it should be added, also contains a number of poems classed by Grierson as "Dubia" and all of these it shares with *L74*; furthermore, these appear in the sequence of poems in the same order as in *L74*. *Dal(1)* is written in a good clear secretary hand which presents few difficulties to the reader, and its existence tends to heighten the authority of *L74* to some extent – because *L74* is no longer the unique exemplar of its own tradition – while at the same time it puts us in a better position to assess the accuracy with which *L74* represents that tradition. In making that last comment, I am of course implying that *Dal(1)* was not simply copied from *L74*; my earlier remark explaining the relation between the order of the poems in the two manuscripts was "a way of saying it", not a literal statement of the actual relationship. I have not yet finally completed my work on *Dal(1)*, but I see no reason so far to suppose that its text is directly copied from *L74*. (I should mention at this juncture that, according to Dr. Beal, there is a copy of *Dal(1)*, which we call *Dal(2)*, also in the Scottish Record Office. I have accepted Dr. Beal's assurance that *Dal(2)* is a copy of *Dal(1)* and have not studied the manuscript myself.)

I must now turn to what I called the internal reason for our need to reconsider the text supplied by Grierson: I mean his adoption of an editorial approach which now seems open to question. In a nutshell, this is his tendency to rely too much on the readings of *1633*. He says that the edition "comes to us, indeed with no *a priori* authority" (II, cxiv), but he claims – rightly – that *1633* is the best of the editions and better than any *single* manuscript (II, cxvi), and in practice his edition is inclined to "save the appearances" of *1633* wherever possible. This tilts the balance unduly against the acceptance of manuscript readings.

It has been argued that since *1633* is largely based on the Group I manuscripts and, where they are deficient, on the manuscripts of Group II, *1633* has little more authority, in a particular instance, than the manuscript tradition on which at that point it happens to be based. Though this has a certain force, it can be, and has been, carried too far. An example – which is, I think, of some interest in itself – will help to make plain what I mean.

The last two lines of stanza 1 of "The Broken Heart" read, in *1633*, as follows:

> Who would not laugh at mee, if I should say,
> I sawe a flaske of *powder burne a day*?

This, as it stands, presents no difficulty: the flask of powder, as commentators have pointed out, is the flask in which soldiers of the time carried the gunpowder for their firearms. The puzzling thing is that, in the manuscripts, the word "flask" has weak and patchy support, with no single manuscript group solidly in its favour – support, in fact, which would make us hesitate to accept the reading if there were any *literary* reason to have reservations about it. The reading which is supported, in an impressive way, by the majority of the important manuscripts is "flash" – "I saw a flash of powder burn a day". (It is worth noting, incidentally, in view of what I say later, that "flash" has the solid support of Group II).

This is not an obviously attractive reading; but a poet of

Donne's stature does not necessarily offer us obviously attractive readings. If such a reading has powerful manuscript support, and an obviously attractive reading is weakly supported, we shall be wise to proceed carefully. Why should so many manuscripts give independent testimony in favour of a reading that their scribes – most of them not averse from using their own judgement in correcting what seem to them to be clearly miscopyings – must surely have found strange if they paused to reflect on it? It would scarcely have been difficult to guess that "flash" was a mistake for "flask".

The answer, I believe one can say with reasonable confidence, is that they were reproducing with some care what Donne was genuinely believed to have written. We are lucky enough to have several examples of Donne's handwriting, notably the holograph verse letter, and from these it is apparent that Donne formed his "k" in a somewhat idiosyncratic way. If you imagine an ordinary italic "k" but with the final stroke of the letter lengthened into a hook which drops well below the writing line, you will have an idea of what Donne's "k" looks like. Now this unusual termination makes the letter resemble to a considerable extent the standard secretary "h", which, as everyone knows, is distinguished from its modern italic counterpart chiefly in having a final stroke which hooks down below the writing line. The answer to our problem, one feels reasonably sure, is that a copyist, or copyists, who were accustomed to secretary hands and to italic hands in which strong secretary features still survived, mistook Donne's "k" for an "h", and perhaps realizing how much more natural a "k" would have been in the context, reproduced what was assumed to be Donne's "h" with particular care, thus no doubt misleading subsequent copyists into the same error. You will have noticed, of course, that this evidence, and the explanation based on it, clearly indicates which is the true reading and which the erroneous one. The explanation will only work if "flask" is the right reading and "flash" the wrong one: it is barely conceivable that a scribe would have made the reverse mistake; he would have no reason either in the handwriting or in the required meaning of the passage to misread "flash" (had that been what Donne wrote) as "flask".

I shall refer to this example again, but my immediate point is that *1633* gets "flask" right, while *1635* changes the reading to "flash", and that is how it remains up to, and including, *1669*. It is instances like this which serve to define the quality and value of *1633*. The compiler of the copy, though like everyone else he makes mistakes, knew a hawk from a handsaw and was not a mere clumsy sophisticator.

But the fact that it is possible to defend *1633* against its severer critics does not furnish us with an editorial principle: we can reasonably treat *1633* as copy text and as an intelligent contemporary attempt to edit good manuscripts into a reliable edition, but we cannot lean on it as Grierson does. What alternative procedures are there?

As a preliminary to outlining my answer to this question, I should like to quote a passage from Philip Gaskell's admirable recent book, *From Writer to Reader*:

> ... the editor should not base his work on *any* predetermined rule or theory. In general he will try to produce an edited text that is free from accidental error and from unauthorized alteration, and is presented in a way that is convenient for its intended readers. Beyond this every case is unique and must be approached with an open mind.[3]

The editor's approach, that is, must be radically empirical: essentially it must be evolved from the evidence in front of him.

What possible principles suggest themselves when one examines the evidence? Some which are theoretically possible quickly rule themselves out: for example, one can no more construct a satisfactory text by relying upon a particular group of manuscripts than one can by relying on *1633*. It is sometimes tempting to imagine that one might trace out, from the mass of material we have, how particular errors have arisen. Here is an example – which I confess amuses me – of the sort of situation I have in mind.

The first stanza of "The Extasie" is almost too familiar to quote:

> Where, like a pillow on a bed,
> A Pregnant banke swel'd up, to rest
> The violets reclining head,
> Sat we two, one anothers best;

That is how *1633* has it. But one of the Group II manuscripts (*TCC*) reads, in line 4: "Satt wee two *on* anothers best" (my italics); that is, it drops the final "e" of the word "one". Two other manuscripts of the group (*N, A18*), together with a manuscript of Group III (*Dob*), take it that "best" here is an obvious mistake for "brest" and read "Sate we twoe on anothers brest", without apparently reflecting that this would be an odd place for lovers to sit. A second Group III manuscript (*S96*) produces the impossible reading "Sate we two one anothers brest", and the edition of *1669* makes a sublimely ludicrous attempt to save the situation with "Sat we on one anothers breasts", which I can only describe as smacking of the *Kama-Sutra*. Curiously enough the Bridgewater manuscript, not known as one of the best by any means, gets very close to the right reading, while not actually achieving it; it reads "Sat we, one, one anothers best", which looks rather like an attempt to bring the reading of *1669* back to some sort of sanity.

But this approach, it quickly becomes clear, will not really help us. It is possible to account fairly confidently for some errors of a simple kind in this sort of way, but beyond that one runs into irresoluble difficulties, largely owing to the amount of contamination between manuscripts even of different traditions. In more complicated instances we may think we see how a given error arose and developed, but we are likely to find that the account of the transmission of the text that our diagnosis implies in one instance is inconsistent with the account implied by our diagnosis of the origin and development of another error.

The point I am making is, of course, that we cannot have our cake and eat it. We must be able to relate our various judgements about what the text should read in places of doubt not only to the evidence concerning those particular places but to each other, and we must do so in ways which maintain an acceptable level of plausibility. In other words, we must have a theory of the text, coherent in itself and consistently applied.

In this, I quite accept, I am saying noting new. But I think it is important to consider with some care how our theory, once we have developed it, can be applied, what it can do and what it cannot. I do not want to say much about the Gardner edition of the *Elegies, and Songs and Sonnets*: I reviewed it for *Essays in Criticism* when it first came out and said my say on the subject very fully then.[4] But I may perhaps take two examples from that edition with the object of showing how, in my view, a theory of the text should be used.

My first example I take from line 67 of "The Extasie". In that line, which usually reads "Which sense may reach and apprehend", Gardner replaces "Which" by "That". The change can scarcely be said to resolve the supposed difficulty of the line, but that is not what now concerns me. Gardner's suggestion is that "Which" was an error for "That", an error which arose because "That" (relative) is often treated in the manuscripts as interchangeable with "Which", and the copyists did not realize that "That", in this instance, was not a relative but a conjunction. But this seems quite implausible on Gardner's own theory of the text. For, as she frankly admits, she reads "That" "Against the consensus of *1633* and all manuscripts" (p. 187). Given the number of manuscripts involved, the variety of the traditions they represent, the contamination between those traditions, the corrections which appear in some manuscripts and so on, can we really accept that there is a right reading here which appears *nowhere* in all the surviving manuscript material? If this objection can be plausibly met in terms of Gardner's theory of the text, well and good. But if it cannot, either the emendation or the theory – on the view I am putting forward – should be dropped.

A second example, of a rather different kind, I take from Gardner's commentary on "The Broken Heart" (p. 173). At line 24 of that poem the Group II manuscripts read "fierce" for "first" in the phrase "At one first blow did shiver it as glasse". Gardner's comment is: "Since *L74* agrees with all the other manuscripts in reading 'first', the reading of Group II, 'fierce', *cannot be considered*" (my italics). Gardner holds that *L74* provides a check on the Group II tradition, which is not an unreasonable view. My point is that a theory should never be allowed of itself to *rule out consideration* of evidence in this sort of way. I should no more wish to read "fierce" at this point than does Gardner, but I would not rule it out solely because my general theory of the text told me to do so. I reject "fierce" for a *variety* of reasons, almost all of which suggest that it is an error.

I cite these two examples because I want to make two points about theories of the text. First, such a theory must inform one's textual decisions all the time: it cannot be simply forgotten about whenever it suits us. When we reflect on the matter, it is clear that our theory of the text is the means by which our radically empirical approach rises from mere preference to principle. Ultimately, of course, the readings we choose express our preferences, but through our theory of the text we accept the double duty of recognizing that particular preferences exclude or entail certain presuppositions about the transmission of the text, and of attempting to be consistent in the presuppositions to which we commit ourselves.

On the other hand, we have the obligation to recognize that a theory of the text is necessarily speculative – though not, I hope, *merely* speculative – and uncertain. It was part of my purpose in citing the *flask/flash* example from "The Broken Heart" to emphasize how liable we may be to mistakes arising from lack of the necessary evidence: if no example of Donne's handwriting had survived, we should not be able to be quite so confident about the way that mistake arose. Our theory will undoubtedly impose certain constraints upon us, and so discipline our thinking. But it is a source of guidance; it cannot dictate. If there is apparent inconsistency between it and other sources of guidance we need to remember how uncertain any theory is.

At this point, I begin to feel that I have perhaps, as the saying goes nowadays, "painted myself into a corner". For having, to vary the metaphor, set the obstacles as high as possible, I now have to try to get round the course myself. But I think you will agree that I have set the obstacles no higher than they have to be. And I would only add that I make the attempt to surmount them in no spirit of easy self-confidence.

What I shall do now is to indicate, in broad terms, my own view of the textual situation in the *Songs and Sonets*, and then try to show how this theory works out in practice when one comes to consider three of the poems in which the variants are particularly diverse and important. I cannot, in the space available, go into detail about my reasons for my view, and I must hope therefore that testing it in the fire of particular examples will suffice to give it at least an appearance of justification. I shall go into considerable detail in the discussion of the particular poems I have chosen to deal with, because it is essential to my argument about editorial practice that one should try to account for everything, or virtually everything.

Following in the footsteps of Grierson and of Gardner, I of

course accept that there are three main manuscript traditions and that, as Grierson says,

> If the manuscripts are to help us it must be by collating them, and establishing what one might call the agreement of the manuscripts whether universal or partial, noting in the latter case the comparative value of the different groups. (II, cxvii)

In passing, I would say that even now there is no alternative for an editor to exhaustive collation of the manuscripts. But what about the comparative value of the different groups? I want to deal with this under two categories: first, the closeness or otherwise of the groups to Donne's original papers; and second, the stratigraphy, as I can perhaps call it, of the three traditions.

Taking the first category to start with, I believe that the Group I manuscripts are in general closest to Donne's own papers. When they make mistakes, these tend to be simple blunders and misunderstandings, rather than sophistications. They impress one as having, so to speak, the authentic Donne flavour and, in common with *1633*, they preserve a considerable number of highly characteristic readings which one would not willingly let go. The Group II manuscripts are careful, and the two principal ones (*TCC* and *TCD*, which are in the same hand) beautifully written. There can be no doubt that whoever was responsible cared about Donne's work and was ready to go to considerable lengths to see that he had a satisfactory copy of the poems. The Group II manuscripts "tidy up" those of Group I in a variety of ways, include a larger number of poems, and add titles for many which lack them in Group I. But Group II does sophisticate (I shall be offering examples in a moment), and I find it difficult to believe that it is as close to Donne's papers as Group I. It seems to me no accident that the compiler of *1633* used a Group I text where he could and only went to Group II when Group I did not meet his needs. Group III, finally, seems much further from Donne's papers than either of the other two: the tradition is more careless; it impresses one as having altogether more errors; of the group, only *S96* approaches in elegance the most beautiful manuscripts of the other two groups (though it could not be claimed that *S96* is the best manuscript of its own group). Yet Group III is by no means valueless to an editor, not least because it often offers significant confirmation of readings in the other two groups.

The stratigraphy of the manuscript traditions, as I have called it, is a different matter. It is associated with the fact that, as scholars are agreed, Donne evidently revised at least some of the Songs and Sonets, and there is therefore a question what readings belong to early versions and what to revised ones. In general, I take it that the Group I tradition represents the earliest substantive version of the *Songs and Sonets* that comes down to us; that Group II represents what may be called a revision, because some of the poems seem to have been revised as wholes by Donne, while there are a number of individual variants in poems other than those revised as wholes which may represent Donne's second thoughts as he looked again at what he first wrote; and that Group III, though commonly closer to the "revised" version, presents a number of readings from an early version or versions of which we have no substantive record.

All this leads to certain presumptions about the significance of agreement between the manuscript groups. We have naturally to remember that any reading, however well attested, can in principle be wrong, and any reading, however ill supported, right. So the questions to be answered are: when particular groups agree or disagree, in what ways are we free to view their readings if we judge them right, and in what ways if we judge them wrong?

When all three groups agree, we shall normally expect some

unusual explanation if we judge their reading wrong: no rules can really be given for this. If Groups I and II agree against Group III, we can take it that Group III, further from Donne's papers than the other two, has fallen victim to an error; alternatively, we can try to argue that Group III preserves an authentic early version, later revised by Donne, or we can take the view that both Groups I and II have fallen victim to an error in transmission. This latter explanation, however, is intrinsically less likely than the other two, because Groups I and II are *individually* much closer to Donne's papers than Group III. If we accept that explanation, therefore, we shall have to give particularly persuasive reasons for doing so.

If Groups I and III agree against Group II, it is open to us to say that Group II offers us either an authentic revision, or an error or sophistication. To prefer a Group II reading in this situation, we shall normally want to be able to argue that revision has taken place, or that the reading of Groups I and III is palpably erroneous.

If Groups II and III agree against Group I, we shall expect to say either that Group I has fallen victim to a copying error – normally a fairly simple one – or that the reading of Groups II and III sophisticates, or that the reading of Group I is an authentic first version and the reading of Groups II and III an authentic revision.

All this leaves us, as it should, with quite a wide variety of possibilities: no possibility can be wholly excluded in principle, of course, but they are not all equally likely by any means, and particularly so when applied to actual variants in the text. I shall now give some detailed examples of how this assessment of the manuscript traditions works out in practice.

I begin with the "Valediction forbidding Mourning". Here, I believe, we can see evidence for suggesting that the Group III manuscripts preserve readings deriving from a primitive version of the poem. Gardner considered that there might be "two slightly different authentic versions of this poem".[5] Detailed collation tends to show that this is indeed the case: to be precise, there is the version of Group III, on the one hand, and that of Groups I and II (which is supported in most instances by the other manuscripts) on the other. The Group III version, about which the manuscripts are in unusually close agreement (the Group III manuscripts are given to disagreement among themselves), was called "Upon the parting from his Mistresse". The principal variants are set out in Appendix 1 below. Where the received version of the poem follows Group III, this is indicated by the printing of the Group III version, which comes first, together with the alternative version. Where no alternative or note is given, the reading is that of Group III alone. Where other groups or parts of groups support Group III in a listed reading, this support is noted, and where a reading attributed to Group III is not unanimous, the dissenting manuscripts are indicated.

First, however, I must say a little more about my reasons for believing that the Group III manuscripts preserve a separate authentic version of this poem. I have already mentioned Gardner's comment, and the internal consistency of the Group's testimony, which in many instances has no support from other manuscripts. It is also important to recognize that all the Group's distinctive readings are acceptable, in the sense that, though we may prefer other, familiar readings, those offered us by Group III cannot be rejected as obvious errors, corruptions, or misunderstandings. There is also Group III's specific title to be borne in mind: on the whole the group is not given to inventing titles – certainly not long ones – peculiar to itself.

The received text of the poem, compared with the Group III version, has all the air of a later revision. If, in the last line of stanza 2 (that is, line 8), the "of" was part of the original version and is not a sophistication – a possibility, since the reading is shared with Group II – it may well have seemed better to remove the word from the revised version, partly because it allows "laity" to be trisyllabic instead of disyllablic (two syllables were possible but may well have seemed awkward) and partly because Donne could then have "profanation *of* our joys" in the previous line without a clumsy repetition of the word in the same place in the line following.

In line 9, I believe Donne may have wished to reduce the original plethora of terminal sibilants, particularly in "Moving*s* of th'earth cau*se* harm*s* and fear*s*", and have felt that he could at least put "Movings" into the singular. But he could not have said "Moving of th'earth caus*es* harms and fears" without at once making the sibilants more obtrusive still, *and* ruining the scansion of the line. "Brings", therefore, solves a problem.

In the last two lines of the stanza, Donne may have felt, by the same token, that "trepidations of the spheres" could do with alteration. If he wrote "trepidation" instead, the line would be improved; the entailed "is" for "are" in the next line would occur unobtrusively in a context free of other sibilants in the immediate neighbourhood; and the jangle of "greater *far are*" would be eliminated. The replacement of "as" at the beginning of line 18 and again at the beginning of line 24 I have no ready explanation for: perhaps Donne came to prefer "like" in this sort of context, or perhaps it is significant that, in both instances, "as" begins a line. In stanza 6 (lines 21–4), it is perhaps not fanciful to conjecture that Donne, on reflection, was not happy with the description of the two souls as "but one", with the limiting implications of "but": "which are one" has a fuller and more positive force which surely suits better with the nature of the poem. The disyllabic "therefore" allows the elimination of "but". And it also strengthens the sense of consequence upon the previous stanza: we are "interassured of the mind" and *therefore* when I go there will be no breach between us. In the following line, the substitution of "go" for "part" is perhaps explicable on the grounds that "part", in its other sense of "be severed", tends to obscure the comparison with the beating out of gold (which does *not* "part") to airy thinness. Nor is there the possibility of a contrastive pun here, if Donne was not prepared — as he evidently was not — to write "Though *we* must part ...", which would have allowed him to set off the "parting" of the lovers, in one sense, with the *non-parting* of the gold, in the other. Finally, "when" in line 30 seems preferable to "whilst" in that it suggests a direct correlation rather than mere parallelism in time.

The spectacle of scholars "finding bad reasons for what they believe upon instinct" — to borrow F. H. Bradley's phrase — is often, I am afraid, more comic than edifying. I hope these speculations have not led me into that trap, and that I have given some plausibility to the notion that the text of the Group III manuscripts represents, more or less, Donne's original version of the poem. For I have a purpose in all this beyond the mere scholarly pleasure of toying with minutiae. The theory I have outlined will in fact help to resolve a textual question that arises later in the poem. The penultimate stanza, in *1633*, reads as follows:

> And though it in the center sit,
> Yet when the other far doth rome,
> It leanes, and hearkens after it,
> And growes erect, as that comes home.

This is the familiar version, as given by Grierson and most modern editors apart from Gardner. Gardner, however, reads — in the last line — "And growes erect, as it comes home". She says, "The agreement of *H40* and *L74* makes me prefer 'it' to 'that'. This may well be a misreading of the spelling 'yt' found in Group I" (p. 190). But further, apart from the editions, Group III and *DC*,[6] the weight of manuscript testimony is overwhelmingly in favour of "it" not "that". Yet "it" is here surely not a happy reading: it makes four "it s" in the same stanza, and what is worse two of those "it s" refer to the fixed foot of the compasses and two to the moving foot; the "it" at the end of the penultimate line of the stanza ("It leanes, and hearkens after *it*") is clumsy enough, but a fourth emphasizes and draws attention to the clumsiness. "That", on the other hand, surely brings out more fully the force of the last line.

If we are guided by the direct weight of the manuscript evidence, or if we feel that the agreement of *H40* and *L74* is really as telling as Gardner supposes, we shall accept Gardner's reading. But there is another point to consider. Assuming one or other of the readings is a mistake, which is the more likely direction of error: was "that" more likely to become "it", or was the reverse more probable. Everyone knows the similarity between "that" and "it" as they were sometimes written in Donne's day, which causes the one to be readily mistaken for the other: "it" is often written "yt" – as it is, in this instance, in *C57* – while "that" is often abbreviated to "y^{t}"; accordingly the difference between the two is merely a matter of whether the "t" is written on or above the writing line – something that is not always easy to determine. I suggest that (a) in moments of inattention one would be much more likely to write a letter wrongly on the writing line when it should be above it than the reverse, and (b) that one's first instinct when reading formal handwriting is to take a combination of letters as a spelt word rather than as an abbreviation, if that is possible; (c) that in the context, there is very little to rouse a copyist's suspicion that in writing "yt" he may be transcribing wrongly; and (d) that "that" is *difficilior lectio*. There is, of course, always the possibility that Donne himself altered "that" to "it"; for the reasons already indicated, I find that hard to believe. But if we judge that he did we shall follow Gardner. On the other hand, if we do not , we shall not feel constrained by the weight of the manuscript evidence to print "it" against our better judgement. For we are now in a position to argue that "that" was what Donne originally wrote and that this is correctly preserved in Group III, that Donne later revised the poem, and that at a crucial point in the course of the subsequent copying a "y^{t}" was converted into "yt". In support of this, it should be said that Donne, on the evidence of the holograph verse letter, commonly wrote "yt" for "it": in the verse letter he does so in lines 8, 43, and 50; and the verse letter also shows that he regularly used such abbreviations as "w^{ch}", with superscript letters, though there is no instance in the holograph of "that" being written "y^{t}".

I want next to discuss "The Flea". I shall not deal with the abiding problem of how we should interpret the poem, though I am tempted to do so, but with textual issues. The principal textual difficulties resolve themselves into three questions: first, were there two versions of the poem, both Donne's; second, if there were, how are they represented by the extant texts; and third, which version should we choose.

Grierson says simply: "It will be noticed that there are two versions of Donne's poem" (II, 36). He does not elaborate, but the grounds for his assertion may be set out roughly as in Appendix 2 below. For Grierson the choice of version is easily made. Version A is that of *1633* and the Group I manuscripts, and so he naturally chooses that version here. For Gardner, matters are less simple: she dislikes the version of *1633* and considers it "less vivid and idiomatic" (p. 174) than the other. Accordingly, she prints Version B.[7]

Looking at the position afresh, one notes that Version B is generally the version of the manuscripts other than Group I and *DC*, and of the editions of 1633–54. This is one of the occasions upon which the bulk of the editions, *DC*, and Group I bear a very close relationship to each other and speak with a united voice: this seems enough to establish Version A as a substantive version in its own right, and to establish Version B in contradistinction to it. Yet there is one point at which this simple opposition is confused: at line 3 "It suck'd me first" is the reading not only of *1633–54*, Group I, and *DC* but also, and unanimously, of the Group III manuscripts. The alternative reading "Me it suck'd first" is essentially the reading of Group II and the manuscripts closely related to it. Unless we give special weight to the Group II readings as such, or to the agreement of *H40* and *L74*, it seems appropriate here to be guided by the weight of manuscript support for the reading of the early editions. On purely literary grounds the case can be argued either way: Gardner says, "The inversion throws the stress where it is needed" (p. 174); Arthur L. Madison says of the other version, "The line opens with an iamb but is followed by a trochee so that the important word *me* is emphasized."[8] It is not without bearing on the decision here that the only other instance in the poem where the division of manuscript testimony for and against the reading of the first edition is similar to this is in the case of the title, which is omitted by the principal Group II manuscripts, as it is by *H40* and *L74*.

I am in little doubt that there are two versions of the poem, that they both go back to Donne, and that the specific readings of the two versions are identified by the agreement of Groups II and III against 1633–54, Group I, and *DC*. In the cases where both Groups I and III support *1633*, the Group II variants do not certainly belong to Version B, and the balance of the evidence strongly indicates that we should follow *1633*. In practice this means that I largely endorse the version of the poem printed by Gardner, but that I differ somewhat from her in my reasons for doing so, and that I do not accept the reading "Me it suck'd first" in line 3.

The third – and for lack of space the last – poem I want to discuss is "The Good-Morrow". Here the position is much more difficult. As Grierson pointed out, "The MSS. point to two distinct recensions of this poem" (II, 10). This view is supported by Gardner and by my own investigations. The most important differences between the two recensions affect lines 3–4 and lines 20–1, but there are variants of some consequence also at lines 10, 11, 14, 16, 17, and 19. One version is represented by the manuscripts of Group I; the other broadly by Group II and varying combinations of other manuscripts. *1633* normally reads with Group I, and since *1633* was the version on which Grierson primarily relied, the Group I text is by and large the text with which readers are familiar. Later editors have followed Grierson's lead fairly consistently. And on the whole, this leads to a reasonably satisfactory text of the poem.

Yet there are possible objections to it. On Grierson's principles, one prints at line 14, "Let us possesse *one* world, each hath one and is one". The testimony of the manuscripts is on balance heavily against this: most of them, including all manuscripts of Groups II and III, read, "Let us possesse *our* world ..." (italics mine), and this reading — I agree with Gardner — gives the required sense of the line. Again, the received version of line 17 seems open to question: it has "Where can we finde two better hemispheares", but Groups II and III, and the editions from *1635* on, agree in reading "fitter hemispheres". Grierson argued for the reading "better" saying:

> The mutual fittingness of the lovers is implied already in the idea that each is a whole world to the other. Gazing in each other's eyes each beholds a hemisphere of this world. The whole cannot, of course, be reflected. And where could either find a *better* hemisphere, one in which there is neither "sharpe North" nor "declining West", neither coldness nor alteration.' (II, 10–11)

There seem to me to be objections to this. In the first place, it is not the fittingness *of the two lovers* that the line speaks of but the fittingness *of the visible hemispheres of their two eyes* to each other. And surely the hemispheres are not "better" absolutely: the line cannot be saying that these are the two best hemispheres to be found anywhere. What is implied is that they are the two best hemispheres *for each other*: this is the whole burden of the poem; the two lovers are parts of a perfect whole, perfectly adapted to one another. The hemispheres, that is to say, could not be "fitter" *for one another*.

As with line 14, then, it is conceivable that the Group I reading was a misreading, at some stage in the copying process, of "fitter"; alternatively Donne himself, on revising the poem, could have thought "fitter" an improvement on "better" for the reasons given. There is, however, a further question: is Grierson right in his interpretation of "Without sharpe North, without declining West"? Is it not at least equally likely that Donne meant – paraphrasing loosely – "We look into each other's eyes and each of us sees one world: those two hemispheres fit together in a mystical union so as to form one world. And they do so because these two hemispheres are so perfectly fitted to each other that they form a *world* even though, unlike the real world, they have no sharp north or declining west." If this suggestion is accepted, the case for "fitter" is further strengthened.

The final point at which the received reading seems open to question is in the last two lines:

> If our two loves be one, or, thou and I
> Love so alike, that none do slacken, none can die.

Long before I thought to question the reading – long before I came to editing Donne – I was deeply dissatisfied with this. We are all familiar, of course, with the idea that what is compounded can die and what is uncompounded cannot. But what has "slackening" got to do with it? The sense in which Donne is presumably using the word is that of "losing vigour", "falling off", "declining" – a sense in which he uses it elsewhere. But what is the significance of "that none do slacken" in "Love so alike that none do slacken"? It seems that "slackening" can only be "losing vigour on the way to dying". But in that case the conclusion will mean something like, "If our two loves are one or thou and I love in such similar ways that they cannot even begin to die, neither *will* die", which is surely weak and diffuse. The whole notion of love "slackening" serves only to flaw the end by a weak anticipation of the real point.

From the other manuscripts, however, we can deduce an alternative version which avoids this objection:

> If our two loves be one, or thou and I
> Love just alike in all, none of these loves can die

The meaning here is plain and, I would argue, just what is required: "if our loves form a single entity, or if, being two separate loves, they are nevertheless indistinguishable, that entity, that identity, that union is uncompounded, without admixture and therefore immortal". Oddly enough, this is the interpretation – though in different words – that Grierson attaches to the "slacken" version: here is what he says –

> If our two loves are *one*, dissolution is impossible; and the same is true if, though *two*, they are always alike. What is simple – as God or the soul – cannot be dissolved; nor compounds, e.g. the Heavenly bodies, between whose elements there is no contrariety. (II, 11)

This is what the alternative version of the lines mean; but it is not a meaning that corresponds particularly closely with the received version. It may be noted incidentally that the following, from Cicero's *De Senectute*, is perhaps somewhat nearer to Donne's thought here than the passage Grierson quotes from Aquinas:

> ... cum simplex animi natura esset neque haberet in se

> quicquam admixtum dispar sui atque dissimile, non posse eum dividi, quod si non possit, non posse interire ... (XXI, 78)
>
> ... since the nature of the soul is simple, nor has in itself any admixture unlike or dissimilar to itself, it cannot be divided; and if it cannot be divided, it cannot perish ...

Donne's meaning seems to find a better reflection in Cicero's "quicquam admixtum dispar sui atque dissimile" than in Aquinas's "contrarietas".

I hope I have made clear the grounds on which I find the received version unsatisfactory. The question now is whether the theory of the text I have outlined will enable us to construct a better version.

In common with Grierson, but in opposition to Gardner, I take the view that the Group I version of the poem represents Donne's first recension. But I also believe that the Group I manuscripts contain certain copying errors and the like. Any given Group I variant, that is to say, may be *either* Donne's original reading *or* an error which has developed in the course of transmission. The Group III tradition I here take to represent, if somewhat imperfectly, Donne's revised text, despite the fact that it appears not to have included the title of the poem, that some of its manuscripts introduce errors of their own, and that its witness to the last two lines is slightly impaired by disagreement between the two branches of the tradition. The Group II manuscripts, like the Group III manuscripts, give us, in my view, the revised version of the poem, but with a number of errors and sophistications, several of them clearly evident, of its own.

On this view, readings which have the agreement of Groups I and III against those of Group II may be presumed to be correct in the absence of evidence to the contrary: in such cases I take it that Group II sophisticates or miscopies. When

Groups II and III agree against Group I, Group I is presumed to be either Donne's unrevised original *or* a miscopying of that original. There is no instance in the poem of Groups I and II agreeing against Group III.

How does this fit the case? First, it is consistent with the fact that the title is to be found only in the Group II manuscripts (and *L74*), in *DC*, and in the single Group III manuscript *Dob*. It is surely more likely that a title would be added in a later recension than that it would be included in the first recension and then accidentally omitted from a wide range of good manuscripts (that is, Group I and all but one manuscript of Group III).

In line 3, we shall assume from the theory that the received version, which derives from Group I, is the original version and "childish pleasures sillily" Donne's own revision: scholars are pretty well agreed in thinking Donne responsible for both. I shall come back to this shortly, however. But it should not be overlooked that in line 4 the Group II manuscripts (together with *L74*) have "slumbered" for "snorted". This I take to be a piece of sophistication. It is not the reading of either of the other two groups, despite their differences over line 3, and I suggest it is an attempt by Group II to produce a reading more consistent with the "innocent" connotations of "childish pleasures sillily" than the familiar, and almost aggressive, "snorted".[9]

In line 10, we shall read "For" at the beginning of the line with the received version because here Groups I and III agree against the "But" of Group II. "But" seems, in any case, to be either a copying error or a foolish sophistication. In line 11, we read "one little roome" not "a little roome" in a situation precisely similar to that which we find in line 10.

In line 13, we read "others", not "other" as in the received version, because "other", though grammatically possible as Grierson rightly said, has virtually no manuscript support, certainly none of the slightest consequence.

In line 14, we read "Let us possesse our world" with Groups II and III (and the overwhelming consensus of the manuscripts) against the editions and Group I. If we wish we can argue that "one world" was what Donne originally wrote, but it seems vastly more likely that "one" in Group I is a copying error for "our": this is a mistake that the handwriting of several of the manuscripts makes extremely easy.

In line 16, we read "true plain hearts", not "plain true hearts" which has the support only of Group II, and in line 17 we read "fitter", the literary merits of which I have already argued, because Groups II and III agree upon it against Group I. "Better" it is open to us to regard either as Donne's original reading which he altered to "fitter" in revision, or as a copying error for "fitter" (not perhaps the easiest mistake to make but a possible one: certainly, I think, one that is more likely than the reverse error of misreading "fitter" for "better").

In line 19, "whatever dies *is* not mixed equally" of Group II is unsupported by either of the other groups, and seems to be the kind of error or, possibly, sophistication which is characteristic of Group II in this poem. From the point of view of sense alone, it appears evidently wrong.

In the two final lines, we shall, on the theory, read:

> If our two loves be one, or thou and I
> Love just alike in all, none of these loves can die.

because the virtual agreement[10] of Groups II and III leads us to suppose that this is Donne's revised version of the original "slack" line, if I may put it like that.

A question arises from all this, however. The theory may perhaps be conceded to give good results in all the instances I have so far discussed, but what about the position in lines 3–4? If "childish pleasures, sillily" is Donne's revised version, are we really to replace "country pleasures, childishly" with this? Though I appreciate the force of the implied argument, I think the answer is "no". As I have argued elsewhere, I believe that Donne is responsible for this revision, but I do not believe he made it on primarily literary grounds. We know that Donne was not happy, later in his life, at the thought of some of the things in his earlier poetry – to the point where, in 1614, he was embarrassed by pressure from an influential person to publish his poems: he writes apprehensively to Sir Henry Goodyer saying, "I know what I shall suffer from many interpretations", but adds lamely, "I must do this, as a valediction to the world, before I take Orders."[11] Everyone nowadays understands the sexual import of "country *matters*"; would not sucking on "country *pleasures*" be the kind of notion that in later life would give him pause and make him consider self-bowdlerization (we can perhaps compare the sort of thing that, according to J. W. Beach, the later Auden did to some of his earlier poems)? It should be noted, however, that the later and – in my judgement – inferior version is not without force. If we assume that Donne's revision read, "But sucked on childish pleasures sillily", the revision expresses the idea of the baby, in its pre-sexual innocence, enjoying the pleasure of sucking the mother's breast: its pleasure is derived from another part of the female body from that which will be the primary centre of attraction for the adult male. And if by any chance the version of *S96* accurately conveys what Donne wrote when he revised these lines, the revision is stronger still. *S96* has "But sucked one Childish pleasure Sillily": the single physical pleasure of the child in contact with its mother's body, as opposed to all the various pleasures of the love-experienced adult.

Nevertheless, the revision is not as strong as the original: it is more restricting and, in the end, less appropriate. I am therefore disposed to offend the purists by producing a version of the poem which, on my own account, may have existed only by parts and never as a whole. I think my reasons for doing this justify such an apparently deplorable proceeding.

Whether they do or not, of course, others must say.

In concluding, may I stress that my primary object in this paper has not been to contest other people's readings, but to articulate a theory of the text and to examine in detail how, in the case of three specific poems, the theory actually works – or fails to work. And this in its turn has been undertaken in the attempt to follow out, as far as time allowed, the implications of an holistic approach to editorial problems, an approach in which one's theory of the text is tested again, by implication, in every textual decision one makes. This is laborious, and it is difficult, but I do not believe that, with Donne's poetry at least, an editor has any alternative, unless he is content to produce a text that is, in Shawcross's words, "eclectic and somewhat subjectively based".[12]

NOTES

1 A particularly clear instance of DC's offering a Group I rather than a Group II text occurs in "The Curse". At lines 14–16 it reads, with *1633*:

> In earlie and long scarsenesse may hee rott
> For land, which had bin his, if hee had nott
> Himselfe Incestuouslye an heire begot:

Whereas Group II and other manuscripts read:

> Or may he for her vertue reverence
> One, that hates him onlie for impotence,
> And equall traytors be shee and his sense.

(It should perhaps be observed in passing, in case anyone should be confused by the apparent discrepancy, that Gardner, in her edition of the *Elegies, and Songs and Sonnets*, Oxford, 1965, p. 164, ascribes the Group II reading here to DC, at least by implication. In fact, it follows Group I not only here, but throughout the poem).

2 There are some examples of this in the "Valediction forbidding Mourning". At line 9, for instance, the accepted version runs, "Moving of th'earth brings harmes and feares". This is the reading of the majority of the manuscripts, and of the editions; but a few read, "Moveinges of the earth *cause* ..." (my italics). DC offers a half-way house, reading, "Movings of the Earth *bring* ...", retaining the plural "Movings" and the plural concord of the verb, while changing that verb from "cause" to "bring". This sort of thing is more characteristic of DC than sophistication.

3 *From Writer to Reader* (Oxford, 1978), p. vii.

4 For the benefit of anyone looking up the review and the subsequent discussion, I should perhaps mention that full documentation will be found in John R. Roberts's *John Donne: an Annotated Bibliography of Modern Criticism, 1912–67* (Columbia, Mo., 1973).

5 *Elegies, and Songs and Sonnets*, p. 198.

6 This, incidentally, invalidates Gardner's claim (p. lxxxviii) that "DC never reads with the editions against both Groups I and II."

7 Version B is substantially the version of – amongst others – the edition of 1669 of whose editor Gardner remarks in her Textual Introduction: "The sources he was drawing on in his endeavour to present a better text would seem ... to have been late representatives of a bad tradition" (p. xc). On one of the comparatively few occasions when one of the Songs and Sonets survives in two versions, however, *1669* conspicuously chooses, in contrast to earlier editions, the version that Gardner believes to be the right one.

8 "Explication of John Donne's 'The Flea' ", *N&Q*, NS 4 (1957), 60.

9 If we try to imagine the alternative priority of the recensions – taking the Group I version of the lines as the revised version, that is to say – we have presumably to think of either:

> ... sucked on childish pleasures sillily
> Or slumbered we ...

or:

> ... sucked on childish pleasures sillily
> Or snorted we ...

as Donne's original. If the former, Donne's revision is oddly handled by the Group III manuscripts, which ignore the large change in line 3 (and what seems to us its obvious improvement) but correctly follow Donne's supposed emendation of "slumbered" to "snorted" in line 4. The latter alternative seems possible, but in that case Group II is convicted of missing Donne's revision in line 3 while introducing a sophistication of its own in line 4. And we have too the somewhat surprising situation of *C57* – offering, on this hypothesis, a text of the *revised* version – being carefully "corrected", not to the original version, but to the intermediate version of Group II. In the transmission of texts, of course, strange things happen, but if *C57* was to be "corrected" here, why was it not also corrected to accord with the supposed earlier version in the last two lines of the poem? This selective alteration seems to suggest some other motive at work than fidelity to Donne's intentions.

10 There is, as I have said, some variation in the testimony of Groups II and III here. One can summarize the divergences as follows. The manuscripts apart from Group II begin line 20 with "If our two loves be one". And in all versions apart from that in *Lut*, *O'F*, and the editions related to them (*1635* on) the line ends "or thou and I". The final line reads "Love just alike in all, none of these loves can die" in all versions except that of Group I, which is here supported by *1633* and DC. Putting all this together gives the version cited in the text.

11 *Letters to Several Persons of Honour* (1651), p. 197.

12 *Complete Poetry of John Donne*, ed. John T. Shawcross (Garden City, N. Y., 1967), p. xxi.

APPENDIX 1

A Valediction forbidding Mourning – Principal Variants

Title: Upon the parting from his Mistress

3 Whilst III; And Groups I and II.

7–8 'Twere profanation *to* our joys (*Dob* after correction)
To tell the laity [of] our love [ ] + Group II, – *Dob*

9 Movings of th'earth *cause* ...

11–12 But trepidation[s] of the spheres, — [ ] + Group I, – *Lut*, *O'F*.
Though greater far, *are* innocent — – *Lut*, *O'F*; + *C57* after correction.

17–18 But we by a love, so much refined,
As our selves know not what it is,

21–4 Our two souls *then*, which are *but* one,
Though I must *part*, endure not yet
A breach, but an expansion,
As gold to airy thinness beat.

28 To move, *yet* doth, if th'other do

30 Yet *whilst* the other far doth roam,

32 And grows erect, as *that* comes home (*Dob* after correction)

Spelling has been modernized; punctuation follows Grierson.

APPENDIX 2

The Flea – Two Versions

	Version A	Version B
3	It suck'd me first	Me it suck'd first
5	Thou know'st that	Confess it
6	A sin, nor shame, nor loss...	... or shame or loss
11	... yea	... nay
16	... you	... thee
17	Let not to that	Let not to this
21	Wherein	In what

To Westminster they hast, and fowly there
Talke plot, conspire, vote covenant, and declare.
New feares, new hopes, pretences new they show
Whilst on ye wondring Towne their nets they throw.
Up rose their Priests (ye viperous brood yt dare
With their owne mouthes their brawlinge Mother tare)
Their walking noysy diligence wee will cease.
They roare, and sigh, and pray, and rail gainst peace.
Up rose ye base Mechanicks, and ye Rout,
And cryd Noe peace, th'astonisht streets throughout.
Here, injur'd Church, thy strong avengement see
The same noyse pluckt downe peace, yt pluckt downe thee.
All strive who first shall goe, who most shall give,
Glocester, and stiffe-neckt Massey to releive.
Their onely Sonns ye frantick Woemen send,
Earnest, as if in Labour for their End.
The Wives (whats that, alas,) ye Maydens too,
The Maides themselves bid their owne deare ones goe.
The greedy Tradesmen scorne their Idol Gaine,
And send forth their glad Servants to bee slaine.
The bald and gray-hair'd Gownemen quite forsooke
Their sleepy Furrs, black Shoes, and City looke,
All ore in Iron and Leather clad they come;
Poore Men yt trembled earst at Finsburies Drumme!
Forth did this Rage all Trades, all Ages call;
Religions, more then ere before were All.

Three thousand hot-braind Calvinists there came;
* Wild men, yt blot their great Reformers Name.
Gods Image stampt on Monarchs they deface;
And 'bove ye Throne their thundring Pulpits place.
Goodwins, and firy Knoxes his brood, ye men
Of bloody Inks, Ravillacs wth their Pen.

To

Cowley's *The Civil War*, III, 33–64, in Panshanger MS. D/EP/F48.

Editing from Manuscript: Cowley and the Cowper Papers

Allan Pritchard

Abraham Cowley's *The Civil War* is a suppressed poem that unexpectedly survived for over three hundred years in manuscript. Written in 1643, it was suppressed by Cowley himself for political reasons and until quite recently was generally supposed to have been destroyed, as his own statement indicated. In the Preface to his collected *Poems* in 1656 Cowley declared that he had "cast away" all the Royalist poems he wrote "during the time of the late troubles, with any relation to the differences that caused them; as among others, *three Books of the Civil War it self,* reaching as far as the first *Battel* of *Newbury,* where the succeeding *misfortunes* of the *party* stopt the *work*; for it is so uncustomary, as to become almost *ridiculous,* to make *Lawrels* for the *Conquered*". The poet, who had recently been imprisoned as a Royalist agent by Cromwell's government, stated that his desire for peace and reconciliation "made me not onely abstain from printing any things of this kinde, but to burn the very copies, and inflict a severer punishment on them my self, then perhaps the most rigid Officer of *State* would have thought that they deserved."[1] During the remainder of his life Cowley did nothing to change the prevailing belief that he had destroyed his long poem on the Civil War. However, in 1679, twelve years after his death, a publisher named Langly Curtis in some mysterious way acquired a manuscript of a fragment, which we now know is a truncated version of the first of the three books of that poem. He published it as Cowley's work, with the title: *A Poem on the Late Civil War,* and he placed at the end the statement: "*The Author went no further*".[2]

Langly Curtis's assertion, "*The Author went no further*", was not disproved until 1966 when I found in the Cowper family archive from Panshanger in the Hertfordshire County Record Office a manuscript of the whole poem in three books breaking off with the Battle of Newbury, just as Cowley had described it in 1656. In the present paper I propose first to give an account of the problems I encountered in editing this long-lost political poem, then to comment more generally on the value for editors of seventeenth-century poetry of such a collection as the Cowper papers, and finally to refer briefly to another great seventeenth-century collection that has relevance to Cowley, the Evelyn manuscripts. My theme is the problems, rewards, and pleasures of working with manuscript sources.

I begin with the discovery of the manuscript of *The Civil War.* This came about indirectly through information I obtained from the National Register of Archives of the Royal Commission on Historical Manuscripts, Chancery Lane, London. While checking through indexes maintained by the Register, I found a notation that letters by Cowley were among the Panshanger papers in the Hertfordshire Record Office in Hertford. This seemed to hold possibilities worth investigating because Cowley had a high reputation among his contemporaries as a writer of letters, but his literary executor and biographer Thomas Sprat regarded his correspondence as too intimate for publication, and only about half a dozen of his private letters were known to survive.

On visiting the Hertfordshire Record Office I found six quite interesting letters, not previously known to students of Cowley. None was fully signed but one had the initials "A C" and there seemed no doubt of their authenticity: they were evidently in the poet's own hand. It was not clear to whom they were addressed, but they were among the papers of Sir William Cowper (1639–1706) and his wife Sarah (1643–1720), part of a vast family archive removed in 1952 from the former country seat of the Earls Cowper, Panshanger, prior to its demolition.

There did not then exist any very detailed catalogue or check-list of this section of the Panshanger MSS, but the papers were gathered into boxes in various groupings. I examined boxes of personal papers of Sir William and Sarah, Lady Cowper, in an attempt to discover how the Cowley letters came to be there and to whom they were addressed. I found no evidence of any direct connection between Cowley and the Cowpers, but in a diary she kept in her later years Sarah mentioned her youthful friendship, apparently in the 1670s, with Martin Clifford, who had been one of Cowley's closest friends and had also been friend and secretary of the Duke of Buckingham. I concluded that the letters had very likely been obtained by Sarah Cowper from Clifford: five were probably written to him and one to his employer, Buckingham.

In the process of examining these papers I found that Sarah Cowper as a young woman had taken a strong interest in the poetry of her period. Apparently she had acquired the Cowley letters as autograph specimens of a poet she admired. She had made her own collection of poetry in two manuscript commonplace books or miscellanies. These included poems by Buckingham (some of which have become known only in relatively recent times from the duke's own commonplace book), Sir Charles Sedley, the Earl of Rochester, and others. In one of these manuscript miscellanies titled "Poems Collected at Several Times from the Year 1670" (now classified Panshanger MS. D/EP/F36) was copied in a fair scribal hand a long poem in three books titled "The Civill Warre", with the note in Sarah's hand: "By Abraham Cowley". It required little examination to establish that this was the poem Cowley had mentioned in 1656 as a destroyed work. Presumably Clifford managed to retain a copy and allowed Sarah Cowper to have it transcribed into her collection. The text of the first book corresponded closely with the one Langly Curtis published in 1679 but had numerous minor variants and a final passage lacking in his text, and there were two additional books that had been completely unknown.

It seemed obvious that an edition of the poem should be prepared. Although *The Civil War* is not as a whole among Cowley's most successful works, it is interesting as being his most ambitious political poem, and constitutes a significant addition to the genre of the seventeenth-century political poem as the only attempt by a poet of stature to give epic treatment to the events of the Civil War.[3] It includes lively polemical passages that enhance Cowley's position as a pioneer of Royalist satire, for example this character of Simon Blore, the woman's tailor turned preacher, visionary, and Parliamentary officer:

> A woemans Taylour once, and high in prize,
> For cheateing with good words and turnd-up eyes,
> Shrill was his voyce at Psalmes, and swift his Quill
> At Sermon-notes more lying then his Bill.
> Thus practis'd long, hee scorn'd the Yard and Sheares;
> Turnd lowd Devine, and taught the naked Eares.
> At last grew Prophet; did strang sights behold;

And much of Beasts, of Hornes, and Weekes hee told.
Till now his zeale to Plunder and the Cause,
Forth to curst warres this various Monster drawes.
A Major there; and none more richly bright,
In silver lace, or better horst for flight. (III.435–46)

The existence of such passages as this provided the strongest reason for undertaking an edition, but *The Civil War* is interesting also for its relation to Cowley's other works. It includes passages that reappear in very different contexts in the *Davideis* and other poems: for example, some of the military episodes in the biblical epic derive from his descriptions of Edgehill, Newbury, and other battles in the earlier poem. Hence when I published in *The Review of English Studies* in 1967 the text of the letters by Cowley, I mentioned my discovery of a manuscript of *The Civil War* and my intention of preparing an edition of it.[4]

As I began to investigate the problems of editing the poem, the excitement of discovery was replaced by less happy considerations, for it soon became apparent that the manuscript presented serious problems. The fundamental problem was that this copy, although it was written in a beautifully regular hand, was corrupt. Sarah Cowper's scribe employed a large clear Italian script and took care to embellish his capitals with elaborate flourishes, but he apparently had little concern with accuracy or sense, and he provided a text that was well sprinkled with errors.

Sometimes the error was so patent that emendation was relatively easy. For example there was reference to "*Bates* large booke" (II.50) in a context where there was no reason to expect the appearance of any character named Bates: obviously "*Bates*" should be emended to "*Fates*". There was a mysterious allusion to "the unworthy seed of factious *Lay*" (II.222), where the historical context suggested that Cowley's subject was the Parliamentary Governor of Bristol, Nathaniel

Fiennes, who was the son of a rebel leader, Viscount Saye and Sele; so apparently "*Lay*" should be altered to "*Say*". In Book I emendations could sometimes be made from Curtis's text of 1679, which evidently had some independent authority. It revealed that the Cowper scribe's puzzling reference to "*Driens*" (I.467) in a description of the heroic death of Sir Bevil Grenville should be changed to the much more comprehensible "*Decius*". Unfortunately there were other words and phrases that seemed equally dubious where the correct reading was by no means so obvious. The editor was left with unhappy alternatives: to print apparent nonsense or to engage in purely conjectural emendation. The difficulty of emendation was much increased by the fact that Cowley as a late Metaphysical poet delights in avoiding the obvious and in surprising the reader — surprising the reader at all costs, his critics have sometimes suggested. Here is very treacherous ground for the editor, where the obvious emendation comes under suspicion as uncharacteristic, and only the unexpected is likely to be correct.

The manuscript had one other specially troublesome feature. The punctuation was frequently very erratic and misleading, so absurd and irrational as to be without precedent or parallel, so far as my experience extends. The problem was not merely at the end of lines (where it is not uncommon for copyists to insert punctuation mindlessly on the principle that any mark is better than none) but at the most unexpected places in the middle of lines: between subject and verb: "I, swear" (II.534); between adjective and noun: "your great, d'signe" (II.540); between noun and preposition: "the guilt, of *Korahs* sin" (II.122); between preposition and phrase: "driven back by, their dispairing steele" (II.127). Clearly this punctuation had to be emended, but one was faced then with the need to make and presumably record a large number of changes from the copy-text, possibly as many as five hundred, and one was left with the sense of insoluble mystery: how to account for such erratic punctuation.

After I had struggled for many months with these textual problems, most of them were suddenly and unexpectedly solved, not through my editorial skill but through the discovery of a second manuscript of the poem. While I had been busy with conjectural emendation the staff of the Hertfordshire Record Office had been sorting and cataloguing the Panshanger papers, and they found in a part of the collection I had not seen three little booklets, each containing one of the books of *The Civil War* (now Panshanger MS. D/EP/F48). They were not so fair in appearance or always so legible as the other manuscript, but it became clear to me when I examined them that they were the original from which the other had been copied. This is one of those cases that demonstrates the validity of the principle for the assessment of manuscripts formulated by the witches in *Macbeth*: "Fair is foul, and foul is fair." The booklets were written apparently in three different hands, one of which was probably Cowley's own. It seemed likely that the whole manuscript in this copy had been seen and corrected by him.

I examined this manuscript with a special kind of fascination as I realized it gave me not only a reliable copy-text but also an authoritative judgement, apparently from the hand of Cowley himself, on the conjectural emendations I had been engaged in making. The efforts of the editor – fortunately still incomplete and unpublished – were in effect about to be graded by the author. The newly found manuscript confirmed my correction of such obvious errors as "*Bates*" for "*Fates*" and "*Lay*" for "*Say*". However, it also revealed errors I had not suspected and solved problems that had been beyond my capacity. For example the scribal copy had a reference to the mortal wounding during the siege of Bristol of a Royalist officer apparently unknown to history: "*Preuation*" (II.249). The new manuscript revealed that this was a scribal error for "*Treuanion*" (Trevanion) who is easily identified. The error had arisen because the form of the "T" in the original was

what helpt these Iron Regiments wth he brought,
that mooving statues seem'd, & so they fought.
noe way for death but by disease appear'd,
Canon & Mines a siege they scarcely fear'd:
till gainst all hopes they prov'd in this sad fight,
too weake to stand & yet too slow for flight.
the furies howl'd aloud through trembling Aire,
Th' astonisht snakes fell sadly from their haire.
to Luds proud towne their hasty flight they tooke,
the Towers & temples at their Entrance shooke.
in vaine their losse they attempted to disguise,
& musterd up new troopes of fruitlesse lies.
God fought himselfe, nor could th' Event be lesse,
Bright Conquest walkt the fields in all her Dresse.
Could this white day a gift more gratefull bring?
O yes! it brought blest Mary to the King.
In Keinton field they mett, at once they view,
their former victory & enjoy a new.
Keinton the Place that Fortune did approove,
to bee the noblest scene of War & Love.
through the glad vale ten thousand Cupids fled,
& chac'd the wandring spirits of Rebells dead.
still the lowd sent of powder did they feare,
& scatterd Easterne smells through all the Aire.
Looke, happy Mount, looke well for this is shee.
that toyl'd and travail'd for thy victory.
Thy flourishing head to her in reverence bow,
to her ye thou owst that fame that crownes thee now.
from farr stretcht shores they felt her spirit & might,
Princes & Gods at any distance fight.
at her returne well might shee a Conquest have,
whose very absence so much Conquest gave.
This in the west; nor did the Northe bestow
lesse cause their usuall gratitude to show.
Candish whom every grace & every Muse,
kist at his birth, & for their owne did chose.
soe good a wit they meant not should excell
in armes; but now they see't, & like it well.
so large is that rich Empire of his heart,
well may they rest contented with a part.

Wth much of fate brave Cavendish issu'd forth,
As swift and fierce as Tempests from ye North

10a

(57)

To duty they order and Law incline,
They who nere err'd from one eternal Line
As just the ruine of these men they thought
As Sisera's was against whom themselves they fought
Still they Rebellions end remember well
Since Lucifer the Great, that shineing Captain fell
For this the Bells they ring, and not in vaine
Well might they all Ring out, for Thousands slaine
For this the Bonfires their glad brightness spread
When Funerall flames might more befitt their dead:
For this with sollemn thanks they vex their God
And whilst they feel it, mocke th' Almighties rod.
They proudly now abuse his Justice more
Then his long Mercies they abus'd before
Yet these the men that true Religion boast
The pure, and Holy, Holy, Holy, Hoast,
What great reward for so much zeal is given?
60 — Why Heaven has thankt them for't, as they thankt Heaven.

— Witness. —

Cowley's *The Civil War*, I, 477–518, in Panshanger MS. D/EP/F48 (opposite), and I, 303–20, in Panshanger MS. D/EP/F36 (above).

not clear and because the middle part of the word was there obscured by a blot. Many of the scribe's other verbal errors were the result of careless response to similar obscurities in the original. "*Decius*" became "*Dreins*" because no fewer than three letters were obscurely formed.

The mystery of the highly erratic punctuation was also solved. The original contained numerous apostrophes as marks of elision, and the scribe had frequently taken these as commas in the line above. For example, the scribe provided this punctuation for a speech made by Satan in a parliament in Hell:

by my great selfe, I, swear,
Had I another Heaven I'd venture't here. (II.534–35)

The comma between "I" and "swear" is an apostrophe taken from "venture't" in the original – in this instance the scribe was careless enough to give it in both places. A similar explanation holds in all the examples of mispunctuation I have given above, while in some other cases ascending parts of letters from the line below were read by the scribe as commas.

As these examples may illustrate, the two Cowper manuscripts of *The Civil War* provide an instructive study in the transmission of texts. The fact that both have been preserved in the same archive for the past three hundred years, and that one is clearly the original from which the other was copied allows an analysis of the origin and nature of various kinds of scribal error with applications extending beyond Cowley's poem to other seventeenth-century texts. My experience in working first with the corrupt copy and then being provided with the much superior original impressed upon me above all an awareness of the limitation of the editor, or at least of my own limitation. I learned the difficulty and often impossibility of reconstructing an accurate text from a corrupt copy. There were many features of the original, including changes in copyists and hands and such accidental features as blots that were beyond my conjecture. In some respects this lesson, I suppose, is similar to the one D. F. McKenzie has taught us about the unpredictable aspects of printing-house practice and the limitations of analytical bibliography as applied to the printed book.[5]

After the discovery of the earlier and better manuscript of *The Civil War,* there still remained a number of textual problems, for example the question of the significance of various cancellations and corrections appearing in that copy, and the question of the relation of the two Cowper MSS of Book I to the text printed by Langly Curtis in 1679 and to manuscript copies of the same part of the poem in the Bodleian and the British Library.[6] But these problems, although sometimes baffling enough, were relatively minor. I could now turn my attention increasingly to the problems of annotation.

The problems of annotation were not peculiar to manuscript poetry but they were intensified by the fact that most of the poem had previously been altogether unknown. Hence one had to proceed without the help of any existing commentary or established tradition of interpretation, although useful guidance to the poet's reading and literary allusions was sometimes provided by the notes Cowley himself had written for the *Davideis* in 1656. Most of the problems were of a kind familiar to editors of those seventeenth-century works that are at once highly learned and highly topical, such as the satires and political poems of Cleveland, Marvell, Butler, and Dryden. Like those poets Cowley constantly fused together allusion to contemporary events with allusion to earlier history and literary tradition, biblical, classical, and English. Authors ranging from favourite classical poets such as Virgil and Lucan to his contemporaries Crashaw and Denham left marks of influence on the poem, and the meaning of the poem was often bound up in the literary allusions. As I attempted to trace these I was frequently reminded of Dryden's comment on Ben Jonson's relation to the classics: "you track him every where in their Snow."[7]

For the elucidation of the topical aspects of the poem as history and propaganda, I was fortunate to have as a starting point not only the notable modern histories of the Civil War by S. R. Gardiner and C. V. Wedgwood, but also the great contemporary history of Lord Clarendon: writing from a Royalist viewpoint similar to Cowley's, Clarendon shed light on much in the poem that would otherwise have been obscure. Neither the modern historians nor Clarendon provided enough detail, however, to explain nearly all the topical allusions or nuances of propaganda. For a fuller understanding it was necessary to turn to the contemporary newsbooks and pamphlets. The answer to most of the questions that arose was provided by *Mercurius Aulicus,* the Royalist newspaper published weekly in Oxford beginning in January 1643, supplemented by the numerous Royalist pamphlets of news and propaganda that poured forth from Oxford in the early months of the war, which have been preserved in the Thomason Collection in the British Library and the Wood Collection in the Bodleian. It emerged, for example, that Cowley's exaggerated picture of a dramatic Royalist "naval" victory on the Thames following the Battle of Brentford (I.325–32), which is unrecorded in most modern histories of the war, quite accurately reflects claims made in Royalist news reports, although such accounts were ridiculed in Parliamentary newspapers. Thanks to the Thomason and Wood collections, I was generally able to provide by way of annotation references to sources published before the end of 1643, many of which were undoubtedly used by Cowley himself. We are fortunate that the first major period for topical English satire and political poetry coincides almost exactly with the beginning of the English newspaper, for without the newspapers we could no longer understand the poetry – no doubt that is a mark of its limitation.

Perhaps the greatest of the problems of annotation was to distinguish between the various strands of historical fact, propaganda, literary convention, and fiction. This may be illustrated by reference to Cowley's treatment of the first Battle of Newbury at the end of his unfinished poem. He begins with a description of speeches delivered to the opposing armies by their leaders, Charles I and the Earl of Essex. Contemporary accounts of the battle record no such formal addresses; evidently Cowley is here following epic precedent rather than historical fact, and some aspects of the speeches seem to derive from those delivered before the Battle of Pharsalia by Lucan's Caesar and Pompey. In describing the king riding about the field of battle Cowley is true to historical fact, but the details of his description of the king's horse derive not so much from observation as from Virgil's *Georgics*, while another description of the behaviour of horses in the battle derives from the *Aeneid*.

Many other details concerning the battlefield and fighting are historical but they are selected and slanted in order to support Royalist claims of victory made in the aftermath of the confused and indecisive action at Newbury. Cowley's statement: "For thowsands then, thowsands of Rebells fell" (III.381) is probably historically accurate, but his emphasis is accounted for by the fact that the enemy pamphleteers claimed that fewer than a hundred members of the London trained bands, which bore the brunt of the fighting on the Parliamentary side, perished in the battle. His catalogue of slain rebel leaders: Swart, Stane, Towse, Ket, Prinne, Frith, and Simon Blore, is evidently fictitious or largely so; the figures must be intended as satiric types rather than actual persons, for these names do not occur in any of the lists of casualties published after the battle; but this remains one of the most puzzling passages of the poem, as Cowley no doubt intended it should, for he cunningly mixed elements of fact with his fiction. In contrast to these satiric portraits, his elegies of the slain Royalists adhere closely to historical fact, and nearly every detail of his long tribute at the end of the poem to his friend, the much loved Lucius Cary, Viscount Falkland, who fell at Newbury, can be abundantly corroborated from historical evidence.

The most rewarding aspect of the labour of annotation was the sense of the recovery of the meaning of the author. Much that at first appeared flat or pointless in *The Civil War* proved to have significance, sometimes very heated polemical meaning, at the time Cowley wrote. Such a line as "The same is *Lord* of *Hosts,* thats *King* of *Kings*" (I.174) falls very flatly until one realizes that it is probably to be read as a refutation of the claims of Jeremiah Burroughes, the celebrated Puritan preacher, who had caused intense resentment among Royalists by arguing in two sermons published with the title *The Glorious Name of God, The Lord of Hosts* (1643) that God had made the Earl of Essex the "Lord of his Hosts". In the case of a work filled with such topical references the editor is faced constantly with the question how to convey the relevant information economically, so as to provide a bridge rather than a barrier for the modern reader and to reinforce rather than distract from the more universal aspects of the poem; but this is among the editorial problems for which I have no illusion that I can offer any solution.

In looking back on my work for the edition of *The Civil War,* from the perspective of a few years since its completion and publication in 1973, one of the most definite conclusions I retain is a sense of the importance of preserving the integrity of such manuscript collections as the Cowper papers that have come down to us from the seventeenth century. If these papers had been dispersed rather than kept together as a collection I would scarcely have been able to move from the letters by Cowley to the discovery of a manuscript of *The Civil War.* Alternatively, if I had found the fair but unreliable scribal copy separated from the other Cowper papers, I might have based my edition on it without realizing that the superior earlier copy existed – an error that indeed I did fall into for a time because the two manuscripts were in different parts of the collection.

Furthermore, if the Cowley manuscripts had not been preserved as part of the larger collection of the papers of Sir William and Sarah, Lady Cowper, I would probably never have been able to provide any answer to the question of the link between the poet and the Cowpers. I had no clue to explain this mystery until in the diary kept by Sarah Cowper in her later years (Panshanger MSS. D/EP/F29–35) I found in a discussion of a translation of Minucius Felix on 19 May 1701 the statement: "About 30 year since Martin Clifford gave me the same translated by himself", and in another entry, on 25 October 1703, a character sketch that showed she had known Clifford well. Here evidently was the missing link, since Clifford was among Cowley's closest friends and is known to have possessed many of his letters, and he had also been the intimate and secretary of the Duke of Buckingham, whose poems and papers figured prominently in Sarah Cowper's collections. When I turned again to look at her commonplace books I found confirmation of this explanation, for the initials "M C" were written evidently as an indication of her source beside copies in her own hand of Cowley's poem "To the Duke of Buckingham" and various poems by Buckingham. Among the losses that would occur the moment such a collection as the Cowper papers was dispersed would of course be the present easy identification of the hand of such a figure as Sarah Cowper at the various stages of her life.

The Cowper papers also provided clues to the solution of one remaining mystery: how Sarah had fallen into the acquaintance of Martin Clifford, who was much older than she was and appears to have moved in quite different circles. In her diary Sarah referred to long residence near the Charterhouse, and among Sir William's correspondence were letters addressed to him at his house in Charterhouse Yard, evidently the location of the family's London dwelling. Since in the last years of his life, between 1671 and 1677, Clifford was Master of the Charterhouse, it seems likely that he and Sarah Cowper came to know each other as neighbours during this period, and that we owe the unexpected survival of Cowley's *The Civil War* to the friendship that then grew up between them.[8]

The way in which Sarah Cowper's various collections and papers are interrelated can be illustrated by reference to other poets, as well as Cowley, whose work she acquired in manuscript, for example Sir Charles Sedley. Sedley is an interesting case because most of his poems remained unprinted until 1702, the year after his death, when the first collected edition was published, and few of them are known to exist in manuscript copies.[9] Sarah Cowper, who seems rarely to have transcribed poems already in print, probably made most of her copies of Sedley's poems from some manuscript source prior to 1702.

In the later part of the same miscellany that contains the fair scribal copy of Cowley's *The Civil War* Sarah Cowper copied in her own hand twenty-seven poems that she ascribed to Sedley.[10] Her copies were unknown to Sedley's modern editor, Vivian de Sola Pinto, but twenty-five of the poems are among those he prints as authentic, while one is among those he prints as doubtful. Her copies contain some unrecorded variants that may be of interest to future editors of Sedley, who is known to have engaged in extensive revision of his work. There is an epigram that suggests her copies may derive from "foul papers" or working drafts that preserve some records of Sedley's revisions. The epigram "To Septimus" (LXIX) is normally printed in this version:

> Thro' servile Flattery thou dost all commend:
> Who cares to please, where no Man can offend?[11]

Sarah's copy has "Thro' servile flattery" written above "For want of Judgment", as if the latter were the author's earlier version.

One of Sedley's songs, "When first *Pastora* came to Town" (XXXVIII) has hitherto been known only in three quatrains, which describe the triumphant career of a country beauty in London. Sarah Cowper's copy has two eight-line stanzas, including an otherwise unknown fourth quatrain, which provides an ironic conclusion to Pastora's career:

> But while she pusht her conquest on,
> Her own poor Heart Pastora lost
> By her so swift success undone
> She can no more her freedome boast.

In addition there is one previously unknown poem attributed by Sarah Cowper to Sedley, twenty-two lines in couplets, headed "To Corrinna Sick Sr C.S: L W.", which begins, "Apollo whose kind influences produce". It has no special importance, but is accomplished and graceful enough to be a not unworthy addition to the canon if the attribution can be substantiated.

Mixed with Sarah Cowper's copies are occasional scraps of information or gossip about the poems and about Sedley himself. Sarah records that the epigram "To Chloe" (LXVII), which urges a lady to cease trying to disguise her true age and to grow old gracefully, was written "To Madame Hall". This is very likely a reference to Betty Hall, the mistress of Sir Philip Howard, whom Samuel Pepys described in 1668 as "a mighty pretty wench, though my wife will not think so".[12] Possibly more important, there is the following biographical statement about Sedley:

> Memor.^le Mr William Ramsey Minister of Pettworth alias

> Thistleworth married S[r] Charles Sedley to M[rs] Askew (tho'is wife was then living) and christen'd their son Charles Ann Sedley. I have had a great do to con: vince my D.[r] of the Legality of the Matter; but I att last convinc'd him with a promise of a Free: School that is in my Gift. This I saw under S[r] Charles's own Hand.

To judge from the version of her hand in which this is written, Sarah Cowper inserted the note at a much later date than she copied the poems by Sedley. The statement if at all reliable has some interest because, although it has long been known that after his first wife became insane Sedley made an illegal, bigamous marriage to Ann Ayscough in April 1672, nothing has been discovered of the circumstances, such as the place and other details given here.[13]

When we turn from Sarah Cowper's literary collections to her diary we encounter another statement about Sedley. She records on 30 August 1701 that she read the news of Sedley's death, for she had lived into an age where one could read these things in newspapers: "The News papers tell us of the Death of S[r] C. S. who hath been infamous for Atheism, but 'tis to be hoped he long since has deserv'd a more favorable charecter. He was a Man of Witt but used it as his own not in the service of the giver". After some further moral reflection she writes: "I have in my custody a prayer compos'd by him, seemingly devout, and a sermon he made to confute Father Elliot, ingenious enough. but with what sincerity he did either, I can make no conclusion."

Sarah Cowper's collections do not yield so much for Sedley as for Cowley, but they provide some textual and biographical information that deserves investigation. Among the questions that will need to be examined is that of Sarah's sources. Sedley was a member of the Buckingham circle, to which Martin Clifford was attached, but Clifford was probably not the major source in this instance because Sarah's collections include poems written by Sedley long after his death. Moreover the initials "M C" never appear with the Sedley texts; instead, the initials "L W" appear more than once. It may be relevant that both Sedley and Sir William Cowper held estates in Kent and that they both served as Whig members in several later seventeenth-century parliaments. The answers to such questions raised by the Sedley material are still to be determined but it seems safe to suggest that whoever investigates the textual and biographical problems will find that they are interrelated and that Sarah Cowper's commonplace books, diary, and other papers shed light on each other.

We are fortunate that the Cowper papers including the diary provide us with so much information about Sarah Cowper, since the nature and value of such a literary collection as hers cannot be assessed very fully without some knowledge of the collector. Born Sarah Holled, the daughter of a London merchant, she married the head of a rapidly rising family of landed gentry, and lived long enough to see her elder son become Lord Chancellor and first Earl Cowper, as well as to see a second son stand a sensational trial on the charge of murder. The diary of her later years 1700–16 reveals a strongly moral character inclined toward Puritanism and afflicted with something of the melancholy that was to reappear in her great-grandson, the poet William Cowper.

The diary frequently sheds light on Sarah Cowper's literary taste and judgment. It leaves no doubt that her reason for including Cowley's *The Civil War* in her collections must have been purely literary rather than political. She can have had no special sympathy for the extreme Royalist views and fiercely partisan spirit of the poem, which in the later seventeenth century would have appealed more in Tory circles than in such a Whig environment as hers. She was so far from converted to Cowley's view of the conflict that she wrote in her diary on 9 July 1701, after perusing another account of the Civil War (in "Colliers Dictionary"), that she "read the story without being affected for either party since both seem to me a pack of self ended knaves that disturb'd honest people who gladly wou'd ha' been quiet." Clearly her primary reason for interest in *The Civil War* was that like many of her contemporaries she admired Cowley above all for his poetic wit. So great was this admiration that not content with having two copies of the whole poem in her possession she wrote out in her own hand a series of witty conceits and epigrams from it in one of her commonplace books (Panshanger MS. D/EP/F37).

In her diary Sarah Cowper claims no great ability for herself as a writer but some skill as a critic. She states on 1 August 1701: "by chance I spell tollerably and that is all. Some how or other I am become pretty able to discern pretty well when others do well...." She makes this comment on the poetesses of her day on 31 July of the same year: "I have mett with none to excel unless ye Admirable Mrs Philips, and wou'd sooner wish my self able to ha' compos'd the prayer we find in her poems than to be mistress of all the Gems, I ever yet saw belong to any Woman. The Dutch: of Newcastle hath made a pudder with philosophy and verse". Here she demonstrates good critical sense in preferring Katherine Philips to the Duchess of Newcastle, but her literary judgments are by no means infallible. She is capable of attributing to Milton and Marvell verse that has little in common with the work of those poets. On the other hand she clearly had access to excellent literary sources, and she had a discriminating sense of what was worth gathering, since her collections include a high proportion of unpublished verse by leading poets of her era: Cowley, Sedley, Rochester, and Buckingham.

Sarah Cowper's copies of poems by the Earl of Rochester show one of the ways in which her collections were shaped by her character. These copies have been unknown to the modern editors of Rochester but they are to be grouped with the texts that today are usually classified as expurgated, although in the past they were often described as free of obscene interpolations. The most bawdy or explicitly sexual passages of such a poem as "Tunbridge Wells" (which Sarah mysteriously ascribes to Richard West) are lacking in her copies. These texts are completely consistent with the picture of her character that emerges in the diary. She was not excessively prudish but she possessed a sufficiently rigorous moral code that even in her younger years it seems unlikely that anyone who knew her would have passed to her copies of the unexpurgated texts or that she would have transcribed them if they had come to her. In such matters as this the character of the collector of manuscript verse is clearly part of the context that needs to be considered by the editor of the texts.

One obvious further reflection arises from the examination of such a collection as Sarah Cowper's: it is that the seventeenth century is extraordinarily rich in manuscript poetry, including much that remains unpublished. There is no complete inventory but some sense of the number and kinds of surviving verse manuscripts is given by such works as Margaret Crum's *First-Line Index of English Poetry 1500–1800 in Manuscripts of the Bodleian Library Oxford* and, for selected authors, the *Index of English Literary Manuscripts* now in course of publication. The unpublished verse probably includes few masterpieces, but it includes poems of some interest, especially in those fields where there were strong inhibitions or prohibitions against publication, such as the category of political poetry to which Cowley's *The Civil War* belongs. For the period 1640–60 there is much scattered topical verse in both manuscript and printed sources that needs to be collected and made accessible before we will have a full and true picture of the development of satire and political poetry in the seventeenth century. One of the editors of the Yale *Poems on Affairs of State* has estimated that almost half of the political satire of the period 1660–1714 is extant only in manuscript.[14]

Even among the religious poetry of the earlier seventeenth

century, a field that has attracted intense modern interest, there is at least one poem of some importance that has never been printed. Sir John Beaumont's "The Crowne of Thorns", British Library Add. MS. 33392, belongs to one of the prohibited areas as a Recusant work, and it has remained almost unknown except for a few short published descriptions and extracts, most notably in an article by Ruth Wallerstein in 1954.[15] Yet this poem is remarkable for its imagery, which displays a quality of sensibility scarcely to be found elsewhere in English poetry unless in Crashaw, and it contains passages in praise of the Virgin Mary that help one understand what Ben Jonson meant when he said of Donne's *Anniversaries*: "if it had been written of ye Virgin Marie it had been something".[16] (Jonson indeed wrote a poem in commendation of Beaumont.) The problem is that "The Crowne of Thorns" is very long and, although an interesting document of literary history, not really a very good poem. Nevertheless, if we are to have many more discussions of Counter-Reformation literary influences on English poetry of the period and many further debates about Roman Catholic as opposed to Protestant poetic traditions and sensibilities, then surely we need to have this poem in some more accessible form. Probably the best solution here would be not a full-scale edition of the traditional kind but a simple transcript, perhaps reproduced on microform or available on demand through the resources of the newer technology.

Whether the unpublished poetry of the period includes any other undiscovered poems by Cowley I do not know, but it certainly includes poems written about him and addressed to him. Two such poems are among the verse of John Evelyn the diarist in a holograph volume titled *Otium Evelyni* in the great collection of Evelyn MSS on deposit in the library of Christ Church, Oxford. Evelyn published little of his poetry, except a couple of commendatory poems, but he was encouraged to write verse by his friend Edmund Waller, as an unpublished letter among the Evelyn MSS shows. Waller wrote to him on 3 August 1646: "if the Muses haue visited you since I left you I beseech you lett me heare of it, yr Lute can only entertain those in the same chamber, but if you touch that other string it may be heard many miles, & you shall be much to blame if you improue not so rich a vayn by adding industry to nature, either that way or in prose".[17] Waller did well to add "or in prose" for, as Samuel Pepys concluded nearly twenty years later when his fellow diarist read some of his poems to him on 5 November 1665, Evelyn's verse is "not transcendent".[18] His talents really lay in fields other than poetry, but his verse helps complete the picture of the interests and activities of the wide-ranging Restoration virtuoso, and the two poems to Cowley have special value in adding to our knowledge of the long friendship between the poet and the diarist.

This friendship apparently began in 1646 when they met in the circles of exiled Royalists in Paris, and developed further in England during the Restoration, when they were drawn together both by their interest in the Royal Society and by their love of gardening. It led to exchanges of visits, letters, and literary compliments, as is well known. In 1666 Evelyn dedicated to Cowley his *Kalendarium Hortense,* second edition, and on 16 August of the same year Cowley reciprocated by addressing his essay in prose and verse "The Garden" as an epistle to Evelyn. He there expressed the desire to see completed and published Evelyn's big work on gardening, *Elysium Britannicum,* much of which survives among the Evelyn MSS, still unprinted, although I understand an edition has for some time been under way.[19]

Evelyn's two poems to Cowley very nicely fill gaps in this record of friendship. As part of his compliment in both poems Evelyn imitates the form and style of the irregular Pindaric ode developed by Cowley. The first was written on receiving Cowley's "The Garden": "To Abraham Cowley sending me his poeme – The Garden". It is an extended celebration in 106 lines both of gardens and of Cowley, which includes praise of his medicinal knowledge of plants and of his literary achievement as the emancipator of poets from the fetters of "slavish Rhyme", as well as high tribute to his general learning, his character, and his conversation: he is a "walking *Bibliotheque*",

> Whose learned Conversation can
> Make any place a *Tusculan.*[20]

The second poem is an elegy written sometime after Cowley's death on 28 July 1667. Evelyn gives a description of the funeral in his diary on 3 August. He may have intended this poem for inclusion in Cowley's folio *Works* edited by Thomas Sprat in 1668, which contained elegies by Denham and two others, although his did not appear, perhaps because he was not satisfied with it.[21] The "Elegie" provides a survey of Cowley's literary career from its precocious beginnings to the *Mistress, Davideis* (of which Evelyn appears to have a good knowledge), and *Libri Plantarum,* and shows once more how much he valued Cowley's tribute in "The Garden". It includes a pleasingly fanciful picture of Cowley's being welcomed into celestial gardens by Pindar and the other poets, while his friend "Orinda", Katherine Philips, prepares the drinks, nepenthe and Hippocrene. This seems a good place to leave him.

The complete text of the "Elegie" is given below, with the permission of the Trustees of the Will of Major Peter George Evelyn deceased.[22]

Elegie

1.

Greate COVLEY dead!
No, he is fled,

I saw him mounte & with his head
Strike the bright Spheare,
And to his Harp an heav'enly Ode prepare;
'Tis Cowleys touch *Apollo* say'd,
Twas he (my Life) or *Pindar* play'd
That Aire:
The God then struck his charming Lyre
Transported with the straine
And answer'd his againe:
Come take thy Seate amongst us here,
We never were 'til now in Heaven a perfect Coire.

2.

But say, may that be death defin'd
When thire remaine no more o'th'kind?
The dying *Phenix* in his bed of fire
Another *Phenix* dos inspire
But our greate *Cowley* leaues no heire
That can our mighty losse repaire:
Iustly we therefore call it death,
So we apply it to our selves beneath;
But to greate Soules, & Pòėts like to this,
Onely their *Apotheosis:*
Pôets like Gods, live every where,
Aboue in deathlesse Soules, & in their deathlesse Poems here.

3.

I say Greate Pòėt: Greate from thy birth
Others are but the Sonns of Earth,
But Thee a Midwife Muse did take
First from the Womb, Yet did not Poėt make.
Thou wert so born
As sometimes Kings are Kings,
And't happens so in onely those greate things;
Whilst Consuls are made every Yeare,
Wise Orators as oft' appeare
But Thou that dignity hast worn
Like those Crownd heads, thrô every Age,

A Cradle Pòët, Child, Youth, Man;
A Gyant, when but yet a Span;
An *Hero*, in *Pindaric* rage:
Never did any reach thy straine,
Never so long did Pòët reigne;
Never like thine, did Wit, and Iudgement dure,
Who hast the heate of both, without the *Calenture.*

4.

Methinks I see how lofty *Pindar* meetes
Cowley, and with his owne high measures greetes,
Whilst *Horace* plays
And *Phoebus* circles both with bays,
(*Phoebus* who envies both their Laies)
The *Muses* with the *Thracian* Bard do go,
The Gosts of *Maro*, & of *Ovid* too;
Dantes & *Petrarch*; *Chaucer*, who th'English led,
And *Spencer*, higher than the rest by th'head;
Tasso, Guarini, Ben, all these,
Conducting him to shady bowers
Tall spreading Trees,
Sweet breathing Flowers;
(And all that in his learn'd **Elysium* grow)
To murm'ring brooks, such as appeare
As his high Raptures, deepe and cleare;
To banks of Myrtils, Ever-greene,
Under whose shade the *Muses* sit,
New Chaplets for his brows they knit
And there his **Mistris* 'mongst the rest,
And there *ORINDA, like a tenth Muse dres't
Prepare *Nepenth* and *Hippocrene*
To entertaine their heavenly Guest,
For thus Greate Pòëts live aboue, thus forever rest.

* *His flora and other Latine poems: on that subject.*

*a poem so call'd

*Mrs *Philips.*

5.

But none dos more our *Cowley* blesse
None more the mighty Name caresse
Than *Isràëls* sacred King,

Davideis.

Whose well-sung suffering
And very Troubles now create delight
Whilst *Cowley* 'in Order dos 'em all recite:
Here he fierce Batells fights againe,
But now he fights them without paine
Nor dos he feare
Sauls Madnes, or his Speare;
Whilst *Jòàb* his greate Acts recounts
To th' *Moabitish* King,
The Carnage of his sling:
How he proud *Philistime* dos vex
And beauteous *Michol* courts;
The *Serinade* under her Window sings,
Set to the warbling of his speaking strings:
His Love to *Jonathan* reports,
Which he in Verse as far surmounts,
As his *friends passion did that of the fairest Sex.

*2 *Sam:* 1.16.

6.

Thy never-dying praise would all surpass
Had I a thousand tongues, & mouthes of brasse
Nor could I halfe thy Virtues summ,
Greate sorrows make us dumb:
Tis we our losses should deplore,
We, who must see thee here no more,
But in thy Books, & art-full lore
And thy perfections to adore,
Whilst thou triumphantly dost sit
A bright, and glorified wit,
In blissfull Regions, 'mongst greate HERO's plac't
Who ways to fame by their brave Verses trac't.

7.

Greate Soule! our Pious Crime remit
If we thine *Elegie* to write
Humbly prophane thy sacred feete
Oblig'd thy Goodnesse to Recite,
When led by mutual Love to Gardens, Thou

*Pindaric on my Book:

Immortal straines didst on our *Worke allow;
A Work that must in every line
Acknowledge all that's Good, is Thine,
The Vegetable World we both declare
Plants the greate *Cowley* claime:
But sacred Laurell none must wth thee share;
To thee *Apollo* first consign'd that care
Which to divulge might we the Grace but name
We would Invoke thy Fame
That whilst full Numbers from thy rich veine do flow
Some Gift thou would'st impart to us below,
Least when to Imitate thy flight, we Sore,
Our plumage faile, & we too-late the rash Attempt deplore.

NOTES

1 Sigs. (a)4–(a)4v.
2 See the Introduction to my edition of *The Civil War* (Toronto: University of Toronto Press, 1973), pp. 6–7. Much of the detail upon which the present discussion is based will be found in the Introduction and notes to this edition.
3 I here follow the Introduction to the edition, p. 10.
4 "Six Letters by Cowley", *RES*, NS 18, 253–63.
5 "Printers of the Mind: Some Notes on Bibliographical Theories and Printing-House Practices", *SB*, 22 (1969), 1–75.
6 See the Introduction to the edition, pp. 61–7.
7 Spoken by Crites in *An Essay of Dramatick Poesie*, in *Works of John Dryden*, XVII, ed. S. H. Monk (Berkeley and Los Angeles, 1971), 21.
8 See "Six Letters by Cowley".
9 See V. de Sola Pinto's discussion of the Sedley texts in his edition, *The Poetical and Dramatic Works of Sir Charles Sedley* (London, 1928), especially I, xxv–xxvii. Several of the poems copied by Sarah Cowper were published in magazines and miscellanies before 1702 but most were unpublished until that year.
10 The poems and the biographical statement given below are in an unpaginated and unfoliated section of Panshanger MS. D/EP/F36. Twenty-six

of the poems occur in a single group, while the remaining one is twice copied in later parts of the same MS. Extracts from the Panshanger MSS are printed with the permission of Lady Ravensdale and the Hertfordshire Record Office.

11 *Works,* ed. Pinto, I, 55.

12 *Diary,* 19 December; ed. R. Latham and W. Matthews, IX (London, 1976), 395.

13 See V. de Sola Pinto, *Sir Charles Sedley 1639–1701, A Study in the Life and Literature of the Restoration* (London, 1927), pp. 128–30.

14 George deF. Lord, in the Introduction to *POAS,* I (New Haven and London, 1963), vii, xxvi.

15 "Sir John Beaumont's *Crowne of Thornes,* A Report", *JEGP,* 53, 410–34.

16 *Ben Jonson's Conversations with William Drummond of Hawthornden,* in *Ben Jonson,* ed. C. H. Herford and P. and E. Simpson, I (Oxford, 1925), 133. A commendatory poem by Jonson is prefixed to Beaumont's *Bosworth-Field* (1629).

17 This letter dated from Rouen is one of nine by Waller bound in the final volume (T–W) of the main series of letters to Evelyn in the collection at Christ Church, Oxford.

18 *Diary,* ed. Latham and Matthews, VI (1972), 290.

19 For the friendship between Cowley and Evelyn see *The Diary of John Evelyn,* ed. E. S. de Beer (Oxford, 1955); letters in Evelyn's *Diary and Correspondence,* ed. William Bray (London, 1854); Sir Geoffrey Keynes, *John Evelyn, A Study in Bibliophily with a Bibliography of his Writings,* 2nd ed. (Oxford, 1968); W. G. Hiscock, *John Evelyn and his Family Circle* (London, 1955); and Arthur H. Nethercot, *Abraham Cowley, The Muse's Hannibal* (Oxford and London, 1931). The MS *Elysium Britannicum* sheds light on Evelyn's relations with other contemporaries besides Cowley who shared his interest in gardens. For example at the conclusion of one section of the work Evelyn writes: "Just as we were finishing this discourse, & meditating what further ornament we might of this kind introduce into o[r] *Gardens,* a most civil lett[r], comes to o[r] hands from the learned D:[r] *Browne* of *Norwich,* wherein amongst other particulars relating to Hortulane amanities, he touches upon *Whispering-places* ..." (p. 172). The letter does not survive among the Evelyn MSS but see Browne's "Echoes" in "Miscellaneous Observations and Notes" and the reference to "the Acoustic Diagramme" in Evelyn's letter to

Browne of 28 January 1659/60, in *Works of Sir Thomas Browne,* ed. Sir Geoffrey Keynes (London, 1964), III, 242–3; IV, 275. Here the *Elysium* confirms Simon Wilkin's suggestion in his edition of Browne's *Works* (London, 1835), IV, 372, that "Echoes" originated as a communication to Evelyn.

20 Evelyn MS. 124, pp. 55–7. The MS includes many marks of revision. In the quoted passage Evelyn has written "roial" above "walking", while "learned" replaces "charming" deleted.

21 Other elegies were added in later editions from 1689 but Evelyn's was still not among them. It is possible that in line 7 of stanza 6 "Books" should be read as a singular, "Booke", in which case it might be taken as a reference to the *Works.*

22 I am similarly indebted to the Trustees for permission to give the other extracts from the Evelyn MSS which appear here. I am grateful also to the librarians of Christ Church for assistance including the provision of some photocopies, with permission of the Trustees. I examined the MSS some fourteen years ago but neglected to make transcripts of the poems to Cowley. The present text of the "Elegie" is based on a photographic copy of Evelyn MS. 124, pp. 59–60. Some minor records of revision appear in the MS. In line 13 of stanza 4 "breathing" is written as a replacement or alternative to "smelling" (?), and in line 15 of stanza 5 "hauty" is written above "beauteous". An uncorrected error is the final numeral in the marginal biblical reference in stanza 5: "2 *Sam*: 1. 16", which should read "26".

Iconoclast and Catalyst: Richard Bentley as Editor of *Paradise Lost*

R. Gordon Moyles

The bulk of our vast store of Milton scholarship justifiably celebrates the author and his work. Occasionally, however, the focus of attention is directed away from the principal towards secondary participants – towards those who, like Jacob Tonson, William Lauder, or William Empson, have shaped, challenged, or changed literary opinion. Perhaps the most widely discussed of these is Dr. Richard Bentley, whose edition of *Paradise Lost*, liberally emended and daringly annotated, has been the subject of a continuing debate ever since its first appearance in 1732. From Jonathan Swift and Alexander Pope, through David Masson and Virginia Woolf, to J. W. Mackail, William Empson, Helen Darbishire, and Robert Adams, Bentley's editorial audacity, his curious blend of critical naivety and perceptiveness have fascinated a long line of voluble scholars.[1]

Primarily, they have been intrigued and perplexed by Bentley's often perverse critical attitudes and with the insights which form the basis of his annotations. Their commentaries have been prompted largely by the view that "he raised several important questions about Milton's use of language"[2] or that, in spite of his wrong-headedness, he provides "an excellent way-in to what matters in Milton's text, and further to what may be called the texture of the poem".[3] As J. W. Mackail more explicitly puts it, "Bentley's celebrated edition ... shows, in large letters, the application and the misapplication of critical method. What is more valuable still, it shows very clearly the width of the field which the application of scholarship to poetry covers, and the mass of knowledge, of insight, and above all of judgement (the fusion, that is to say, of imagination and common sense) which it demands."[4] Clearly, that argument has been exhaustively, even if not always satisfactorily, dealt with: I will add nothing further to it.

There is, however, in nearly all the preceding commentary, either an implicit or explicit assumption that Bentley was, though ambivalent in his critical approach, both diligent and acute in his treatment of the text. In this the commentators are clearly mistaken – mistaken because they have not examined the textual history of *Paradise Lost*. In her 1952 James Bryce Lecture, for example, Helen Darbishire incautiously maintained that Bentley had "carried through a relentless scrutiny of the text" and had "carefully collated" the manuscript of Book I. She and almost every other commentator have mistakenly given Bentley credit for the judicious (and now universally accepted) emendation at VII.451 ("foul" to "soul"), unaware of the fact that it originated with Patrick Hume as early as 1695. J. W. Mackail, in fact, cites that emendation as proof of Bentley's "genius" as a textual critic which, he asserts, here "shows itself most conspicuously".[5] Just as clearly, then, this aspect of the Bentleian commentary – Bentley's textual awareness and editorial acumen – demands a more thorough and rigorous investigation.

It is my intention, therefore, to do just that – to assess Bentley's editorial achievement against that of his predecessors, and to find out just how much he knew about the authoritative originals and the variants between them. I will suggest that Bentley's contribution to the textual progress of *Paradise Lost* rests not on his "genius as a textual critic" or on one or two universally accepted emendations, but on the unintended influence of his editorial audacity. Contrary to his expectations, his charges of spuriousness and his policy of liberal emendation prompted subsequent editors and scholars to pursue textual fidelity; reacting strongly against Bentley's "immodest proposals", they began to search out the facts, collate the authoritative texts, and thereby lay the groundwork for the first definitive edition of the poem. In other words, I hope to demonstrate that, even though Bentley's handling of the text was extremely casual – inferior in many respects to that of some of his less enlightened contemporaries – he was nevertheless the catalytic agent of textual reform.

In 1732 *Paradise Lost* was entering its sixty-fifth year of publication; both the poem and its author were by now "revered" and the English reading-public had created such a demand for it that there existed fifteen complete editions – large handsome folios, unprepossessing quartos and octavos, pocket-sized duodecimos – in varying degrees of refinement. All except two of these, the 1678 third edition (published by Samuel Simmons) and a pirated edition out of Dublin in 1724, were produced by the family of England's "prince of publishers", Jacob Tonson, who purchased the rights to the poem in 1683. In 1688, 1691, and 1695 Tonson honoured Milton by publishing three magnificent and expensive folios, the first containing John Baptist Medina's famous "sculptures" and the last being accompanied by Patrick Hume's lengthy *Annotations*; in 1705, 1707, and 1711 Tonson capitalized on the increasing popularity of *Paradise Lost* among the so-called "ordinary" English readers and produced cheaper octavos and duodecimos; in 1719 he hired his first official editor, John Hughes, who was followed by Thomas Tickell for the 1720 deluxe edition, and by Elijah Fenton who prepared the editions of 1725, 1727, and 1730.

It would, of course, in view of what we know about eighteenth-century editorial procedures, be naive to expect either Tonson or his editors to have paid any attention to textual fidelity. Like most other editors of their day they were primarily concerned to produce refined rather than definitive editions; thus each edition of *Paradise Lost* was based on an immediately preceding one, thereby perpetuating previous corruptions and, by introducing fresh errors, causing the text of the poem to deviate progressively from the two authoritative originals of 1667 and 1674.

Significantly overlooked, therefore, either deliberately or through the inaccessibility of original texts, were the variants within and between those two authoritative editions, the only two overseen by Milton himself. The first edition, though printed entirely in 1667 from a single setting-up of type, contained variants in sixteen of its eighty-six formes and existed with six different title pages, two each for 1667, 1668, and 1669.[6] Early editors were so unfamiliar with these various issues that, as late as 1727, Elijah Fenton was mistakenly listing 1669 as the date of first publication. More textually important, but equally unknown, was the state of the second "revised" edition of 1674. That it had been redivided into twelve books (from ten), necessitating a number of major revisions, was made widely known by Joseph Addison in his 1712 *Critique*; that there were, in addition, more than eight hundred other variants, approximately forty of them substantive, remained largely undiscovered for another four decades. If the second edition were superior to the first in every instance, the failure to collate the two would have mattered little; but for more than one-third of the variants the first edition is superior and for another third, where the choice of superior reading is not obvious, reasoned editorial eclecticism must be practised. Such matters, however – the question of copy-text, the need for careful collation, the eclectic treatment of variants – were not among the early eighteenth-century publisher's priorities and did not unduly concern Jacob Tonson or his editors.

This does not mean, of course, that no textual progress at all was made by the first editors of *Paradise Lost*. The unknown editor of the 1695 sixth edition, for example, recovered several superior Quarto readings and the editor of the seventh (1705) undertook a careful scrutiny of his copy-text (the 1695), thus ridding his own text of many perpetuated corruptions.[8] More impressively, the first known editor of *Paradise Lost*, John Hughes, who prepared the 1719 edition, seems to have used a 1667 text as a casual correcting copy, thereby retrieving several more superior Quarto readings. Had Hughes adopted either the 1667 or the 1674 as his copy-text, instead of the notorious 1711 edition, he might have set the text well on its way towards definitiveness; but the little progress made by him was nullified by that choice, for the 1711 was riddled with errors, had perpetuated all previous corruptions, and had introduced more than twenty-five fresh emendations. And it was that sort of editorial procedure – the preference of immediately preceding editions as copy-texts and a failure to collate the authoritative originals – which had thus far thwarted textual progress. That, plus an obvious reliance on intuitive correction and an even more obvious predilection for conjectural emendation.

At X.550, for example, the 1667 edition of *Paradise Lost* reads: "Thir penance, lad'n with fair Fruit, like that". In the 1674 edition "fair" is omitted, thus rendering the line metrically deficient. The unknown editor of the 1695 edition noticed the deficiency, but since he was not aware of the authoritative version he intuitively corrected the line to read:

"Their penance, lad'n with Fruit, like to that". The 1711 editor copied the 1695 emendation and, for some obscure reason, emended the line further to read: "Their patience, lad'n with Fruit, like to that". Every subsequent edition to 1730 reads the same. When, in fact, Elijah Fenton assumed the editorship of the 1725, 1727, and 1730 texts he threw editorial caution to the wind and introduced, unannounced, more than a hundred barbarous emendations. These, combined with the many already perpetuated through the twelve editions since 1688, meant that the 1730 text, the last before Bentley's, was considerably removed from the authoritative originals and, in some instances at least, was hardly recognizable as being Milton's.

It would be decidedly unfair, however, to condemn Elijah Fenton or to judge his editorial performance by present-day standards. He was by no means alone in his espousal of liberal emendation; in the early part of the eighteenth century "conjectural criticism" had become the "darling passion" of many other scholars who, like Lewis Theobald, declared themselves to be "avaricious husbandmen" of emendations.[9] And they were, for the most part, the disciples of Dr. Richard Bentley – the foremost classical scholar of his day and the acknowledged "father of conjectural criticism" – whose emendatory skills had been perfected and amply displayed in his editions of Horace, Terence, and later Manilius. An editor's task, Bentley maintained, was to "restore" his text – to ascertain error by intuition (based on experience in reading the classics) and to invent, by sagacity, plausible emendations. In his edition of Horace he summed up his editorial method by stating, in effect, that he "considered conjecture more certain than manuscript reading, and the reason and the sense of the passage itself stronger than a hundred manuscripts".[10] On the whole, the conjectural method served the classics well, for Bentley seemed gifted (as De Quincey put it) "with an intuitive sagacity" which, in spite of an unprecedented amount of pure conjecture, enabled him to restore the exact sense to many puzzling passages – a feat which won him considerable admiration, though there were, among his critics, some who deplored his "predilection for conjecture beyond reasonable limits".[11]

It is not surprising to learn, then, that when Bentley decided, or was persuaded, to edit *Paradise Lost* (his first editorial encounter with an English text) he proceeded to do so according to the proven principles of conjectural criticism. And, being the master, he naturally outstripped his disciples in both daring and ingenuity. He first of all assumed (or perhaps was forced by his editorial method to assume) that the existing text, in both original editions, was so corrupt – indeed, contained faults as were "beyond example in any other printed book" – that only liberal emendation, accomplished by "sagacity and happy conjecture", would "retrieve the poet's own words". He would not, however, like previous editors, silently emend his text but would "let the purchaser know what he is to expect in this new Edition" by casting his emendations into the margins, "so that every reader has his free choice, whether he will accept or reject what is here offer'd him". In other words, his would be the first critical edition of the poem – with both critical introduction and textual apparatus – the text of which, he firmly asserted, would be "the truest and correctest that has yet appear'd".

The confused and contradictory nature of Bentley's stated procedure is obvious enough and it is just this sort of contradiction – coupled with inconsistency and carelessness – which is the hallmark of his editorial treatment of *Paradise Lost*. Bentley will, for example, make and defend choices between Quarto and Octavo readings, in spite of the fact that he insists that neither is authoritative. He could, it is clear, have apprised his readers of the existence of the Manuscript of Book I – then in Jacob Tonson's possession – for there is ample evidence that he used it in a casual way, but his rigid editorial position forces him to deny its existence. He could, moreover, have profited by a careful collation of the Quarto and Octavo texts, for again there is evidence that he was acquainted with them, but he chooses not to do so. Instead, he uses a copy of the 1720 edition as his copy-text, correcting it sometimes by intuition, sometimes against the manuscript, sometimes (but not often) against the first edition, and, curiously, sometimes even against a copy of the 1725 edition.[12] Quite clearly, working in such a piecemeal fashion, Bentley is not always certain when he is dealing with authoritative readings and when he is not.

At II.568 and V.42, for example, Bentley unknowingly adopts incorrect readings which had originated with the editions of 1688 and 1711; at III.592, VI.345, VI. 797, and IX.347 he (again unknowingly) copies the errors of his copy-text; at X.392, XI. 344, and XI.583 he offers correct Quarto readings as emendations, obviously unaware that they are authoritative; and at II.91, where the 1720 edition correctly reads "inexorably", Bentley silently adopts "inexorable", the incorrect 1725 reading. Even when Bentley makes seemingly judicious editorial decisions, we find that his sources are external to the text. The celebrated emendation of "foul" to "soul" (VII.451) is, as I have already mentioned, found as early as 1695 in the *Annotations* of Patrick Hume. Similarly, his much-applauded choice of "founded" (instead of "found out") was quite likely the result not of collation but of its being discussed in the *Grub-Street Journal* of June 1730.

On the basis of such evidence (which could be multiplied if space permitted), one is justified in concluding that Bentley did not carefully collate or even scrutinize the authoritative editions; that his text, not surprisingly, is far from being "the truest and correctest" yet produced; that his editorial treatment is in no way superior to that of Elijah Fenton and his text is, in fact, inferior to both the 1705 and 1719 editions; and, finally, that the edition of 1732, devoid of its marginalia

– its eight hundred emendations and the accompanying commentary – would have been, though a handsome folio edited by a famous scholar, merely one edition among many, textually insignificant and, like most of its contemporaries, now virtually forgotten. It was not Bentley's text but his textual apparatus which, in a manner Bentley did not expect, provided the stimulus to textual progress.

Bentley's determination to "retrieve the Poet's own words ... by Sagacity and happy Conjecture", resulted, as I have already mentioned, in a great deal of contradiction and confusion. It not only forced him to deny the existence of a manuscript but, more significantly, also forced him to concoct an elaborate fiction regarding the printing of the poem. To account for the "corrupt" state of the existing texts, he invented a "phantom editor" – "an injudicious smatterer in Astronomy, Geography, Poetical Story, and Old Romances", who not only added to the errors of the printer, but who foisted on the text numerous inventions of his own. "If," Bentley argued, "any fancy this *Persona* of an Editor be a mere Fantour, a Fiction, an Artifice to Skreen Milton himself, let him consider these four and sole changes in the Second Edition." In support he quotes the four major revisions, the most offensive (for him) being that at XI.485:

> Daemonic Phrenzie, moaping Melancholie
> And moon-struck madness, pining Atrophie,
> Marasmus, and wide-wasting Pestilence.

"But now," he continues, "if the Editor durst insert Forgeries, even in the Second Edition, when the Poem and its Author had slowly grown to a vast reputation, what durst he not do in the First, under the Poet's Poverty, Infamy, and an Universal Odium ...?" The answer to that question was, quite obviously, "almost anything", for Bentley insists that such monstrous faults were committed by him "as are beyond examples in any other printed book".

"What an idiot of an Editor," cries Bentley in his note to VII.463, where he declares the following twelve lines to be merely a spurious insertion:

> The grassie Clods now calv'd, now half appear'd
> The tawny lion, pawing to get free
> His hinder parts; then springs as broke from bonds,
> And rampant shakes his brinded main. The Ounce,
> The Libbard, and the Tiger, as the Mole
> Rising, the crumbl'd Earth above them threw
> In hillocks. The swift Stag from under ground
> Bore up his braunching head. Scarce from his mould
> Behemoth, biggest born of Earth, upheav'd
> His vastness. Fleec'd the Flocks and bleating rose,
> As plants; ambiguous between Sea and Land
> The River Horse and scaly Crocodile.

"Here we come," Bentley vociferates, "to a whole Dozen of Verses, which are demonstrably an Insertion of the Editor's, without the Poet's knowledge.... Calv'd is a Metaphor very heroical, especially for wild Beasts. But has not the Author express'd it, and much better, before?

> 'The Earth obey'd, and straight,
> Op'ning her fertil Womb teem'd at a Birth.'

"Would a man, that had once said *teem'd*, have doubled and polluted it with *calv'd*? He goes on, *The Lion pawing to get free his hinder parts*. The poor Lion stuck fast in the Passage; he was form'd, it seems, in the Earth, without any Cavity for him. And his hinderparts being much thinner than his fore-parts: if these were once out, he needed not to paw and struggle to get free the *hinder ones*, which could not possibly stick at all."

In like manner, with extreme literal-mindedness, Bentley proceeds to dismiss the remainder of the "spurious" passage. And in seventy-five other instances he repeats his charge: the coupling of pagan and divine themes (as at IV.705-7), the long lists of historical and mythological names (as at X.524 ff.), the mention of "Uther's son begirt with British and Amoric knights", and the famous description of the Paradise of Fools in Book III are all seen to be beneath the poetic dignity of Milton, not in keeping with his lofty purpose, and therefore the result of editorial interference. Bentley would expurgate them completely from his text.

And what he does not reject, Bentley emends. Attempting to reconcile "high language with philosophy and true sense", he battles with tautologies, regularizes the metre, denounces internal rhymes, and generally turns good poetry into bad prose. The following few examples provide illustrations of Bentley's emendatory methods and his "common sense" reasoning:

> I.157 To be weak is miserable.] The printer here has bestowed upon our poet absolute nonsense. To be weak is not by consequence to be *miserable*. Adam was *frail* and *weak*, even while he was happy in Paradise. But it's no answer to Belzebub's speech. He complain'd not of *Weakness*; on the contrary, he own'd that vigour was return'd, and their *strength was undiminish'd*: but he doubted what God's design was in placing them in *Hell*, whether they should work for him, or merely *suffer* pain. That either way, *working* or *suffering*, 'twas miserable for them to *live* in *Hell*. The author therefore gave it, to be *Here is miserable*. Or rather thus, *Fall'n Cherub*, here to *dwell is miserable*.

> I.282 Fall'n such a pernicious Highth.] Fall'n a highth is not Common Sense: and a *pernicious Highth* is not a

whit better. The Poet gave it, *No wonder, fall'n from such prodigious Highth*.

V.198 Ye Birds, that singing up to Heaven-Gate ascend.] The Sky Lark sings as she ascends; perhaps no other bird. But to ascend to Heaven Gate, which Milton always places above the sphere of fix'd stars, is out-stretched beyond possibility. He gave it thus: *That soaring up to Heavenward ascend.*

V.293 And flouring Odors.] *Odorous Flours* is common sense and language; but *flouring odours* is affectation extravagant. I suspect he gave it, nor are the letters very remote, *Ambrosial odors*.

On more than eight hundred other occasions Bentley proposes similar emendations – sometimes whole lines, often only single words – to suit his own tastes and his ideas of classical decorum. From Book I, line 6, where he conjectures that "secret" should be "sacred", to the last two lines of the poem, which he proposes should read

> Then hand in hand with social steps their way
> Through Eden took with Heavenly comfort cheer'd

Paradise Lost has been subjected to an excess of conjectural criticism. "The rage of conjecture seems to have seized him," wrote John Harris, "as that of *Jealousy* did *Medea*; a rage, which she confest herself unable to resist, altho' she knew the mischief it would prompt her to perpetrate."[13]

It should not be said that Bentley's emendations came as a great surprise to the English literary community, especially to devotees of Milton. For more than two years they had been aware of Bentley's plans; he had already published an "Essay to Defend a Critical Emendation of Paradise Lost"

(1731) and had made public a few of his choice alterations, notably the change of "secret" to "sacred". And already the *Grub-Street Journal* had denounced and satirized Bentley's methods and conjectural criticism in general.[14] But it was only when the edition appeared in the Fall of 1732, when the proposal became a reality and the full extent of Bentley's editorial audacity became evident, that the "defenders of Milton" raised their voices in loud and hostile protest.

At first, still in 1732, the outcry, confined primarily to the *Grub-Street Journal* and small pamphlets, was just that – a cry of outrage, attended by a few witty rejoinders, satirical jibes, and clever parodies. Bentley, one writer facetiously suggested, simply had not gone far enough and he quoted Book IV, line 677, offering a Bentleian emendation in jest:

> "Millions of spiritual creatures walk the earth" – Indeed! Millions! So many could not walk together in Paradise, which the Author must mean by earth, unless "gods met gods, and jostled in the dark". Besides, so many singers would quite deafen Adam and Eve, or else deprive them of all sleep and distract them. Read it, therefore, as the author gave it, *Several.*

The same satirical tone, a mixture of burlesque and banter, lacking in scholarly argument, pervaded the entertaining 64-page pamphlet entitled *A Friendly Letter to Dr. Bentley*, the spirit of which is exhibited in the following passages:

> I.63 No light but rather Darkness Visible.] (you cry out) *A Flat Contradiction*, which you prove unanswerably from Sir Isaac Newton's Treatise on Light and Colours. Ah, these Poets, these Poets, with their bold Figures and Flights, and all that, I'gad, do often leave us in the Dark; Hey, Doctor. We thank you therefore my dear Friend, for affording us a little *Light*, by altering *visible Darkness*

to a *transpicuous Gloom*; which word *Gloom*, you say, is *equivalent to darkness, yet so as to be in some measure transparent*. Ha! Ha! delightful! So that a *transpicuous gloom* is a *transpicuous transpicuity*.

II.631 Puts on Swift Wings.] This is a merry Blunder, you say, of the Printer or Editor; as if Satan had no natural wings of his own, but was forc'd, like Daedalus, to put some on: You are therefore for reading it, Put on swift-wing'd. Here, I doubt, the Adversary will be apt to aver, that this is a merry Blunder of the sagacious Dr. Bentley, who cold not plainly see that Milton's Expression was metaphorical, and meant nothing else than moving forward swiftly with his Wings. To which we must answer, that we do by no means allow of the metaphorical way of speaking.

VI.237 No unbecoming Deed, that argu'd Fear.] *Deed*, you here desire may be chang'd into *Flinch*, for 'tis want of Deeds, you say, that argues *Fear*. Here Doctor, I think you ought at least to have given us a Dissertation upon a *Flinch*, and inform'd us what kind of *Flinches* were *becoming*, and *argu'd Courage*, and what were *unbecoming* and *argu'd Fear*, for now I doubt we shall not be able to know an *unbecoming Flinch* from any other, because all Flinches have hitherto been deem'd *unbecoming* alike.

In *Milton Restor'd and Bentley Depos'd* (1732) the putative author Dean Swift, who coined his own motto, "Sing Heav'nly Muse, from Pedantry be Free", also depended largely on satire and parody to ridicule Bentley's achievement. "I confess," he wrote in pure Bentleian style, "I am so stonish'd, stonied, and stunn'd with the arrogance and impertinence of the Doctor's Emendations, that I have scarce patience to read them." Read them he did, however, and, like the *Grub-Street Journal* critics, he attacked Bentley's logic, chided his lack of poetic sensitivity – calling him a "Grammarian, whose trade lies in Genders, Moods, and Tenses, who cannot dispense with excellence beyond a Rule, nor suffer a Grace to remain which is not obedient to Construction" – and, finally, offered the reader an example of what else could still be done to render *Paradise Lost* more readable:

> Of man's first Breach of the Divine Decree,
> And the fair Fruit of that Forbidden Tree,
> Whose mortal Taste the World's great ruin wrought;
> And Sin and Death, and loss of Eden brought;
> Till Sin and Death one greater man defeat,
> Restore us, and regain the blissful Seat.
> Sing Heav'nly Muse, that veil'd from Human View
> On Oreb's Top, or Sinai's lofty Brow,
> Didst first inspire the Shepherd to disclose
> How Heavens and Earths from Dusky Chaos rose.

It is not surprising, of course, to find these front-line defenders resorting to caustic satire and witty burlesque; it was, by and large, the manner Bentley himself had employed when ridiculing his fictitious editor. Reasoned defences, supported by scholarly argument, took time to prepare – they came only after the smoke of the early battle had cleared.

The first of these, and perhaps the best, was Zachary Pearce's four hundred pages of erudite reasoning entitled *A Review of the Text of Paradise Lost* (1732; rev. 1733), in which he quietly demolished most of Bentley's arguments. More significant to us is the fact that Pearce begins, rather shakily, to explore the text itself. In the 1732 version of his *Review* he affirmed that the first edition of *Paradise Lost* had been published in 1669; in the 1733 version he revised that statement, going on to state that there were three title-pages for the first edition even though there seemed to be but "one impression in Quarto".

In 1734 the Jonathan Richardsons (father and son), in their *Explanatory Notes and Remarks on Milton's Paradise Lost*, supported Pearce's statement, stating in turn that they had seen six copies of the first edition:

> Fenton tells us that the Book was first Publish'd 1669. Others have thought so too; and 'tis true there are of the First Quarto Editions with that Year in the Title-page. The Case is Thus; there are Three several Titles with a little Variation in Each, besides That of the Date; there are of 67, and 68, as well as of 1669. The Same Sheets, only a Word and a Point or two alter'd, the Sheet Otherwise the Same, not Cancell'd, but the Alteration made as 'twas Printing (p. cxvi).

The Richardsons also perused the second edition of *Paradise Lost* and found it to be so thoroughly in agreement with the first that "we have reason to assure our Selves, especially if we take Both These Authentick Editions together, that we are in Possession of the Genuine Work of the Author as much as in Any Printed Book whatsoever." The only three emendations which could be accepted, they argued, were "swelling" (VII.321), "Soule" (VII.451), and "me" (IX.1019), the last being, though the Richardsons did not know it, the correct Quarto reading. "So," they advised Bentley, "Go thy Ways, the Flour and Quintessence of all Editors, the edition of 1674 is the Finish'd, the Genuine, the Uncorrupted Work of John Milton" (p cxxxciii).

Taking the Richardsons to task for what he felt to be but a cursory scrutiny of the authoritative editions, Francis Peck, in his *New Memoirs of the Life and Poetical Works of Mr. John Milton* (1740), produced what is, to all intents and purposes, the first list of variants ever compiled:

> [After listing the three accepted by the Richardsons, he states:] Yet I will venture a few more: viz. II.483. her, for thir. II.702. stroc, for stroke. II.1039. brok'd, for brok'n. III.592. medal, for metal. III.597. to, for or. III.716. this, for the. IV.136. gottesque, for grotesque. IV.226. mould, for mound. IV.751. offsspring, for off-spring. IV.956. acknowldg'd, for acknowledg'd. VII.63. conspicious, for conspicuous. IX.1092. from, for for. 1093. for, for from. X.997. meserie, for miserie. XI.798. loose, for lose. XII.534. well, for will.

The fact that Peck's scrutiny of the text was little superior to the Richardsons' – that four of his supposed variants are in fact conjectural emendations and most of the others mere typographical errors – is not a serious matter. What is more obviously important is the fact that the text of *Paradise Lost*, thanks to Bentley's perverse prompting, is being examined. Apart from his list of variants, Peck offers a list of editions which includes every edition up to 1732, plus the three issues of the first edition, and provides quasi-facsimile title-pages for both the Quarto and Octavo texts. And in Chapter 24 of his *New Memoirs* he corrects Elijah Fenton's 1725 edition against the 1674 as an illustration of the kind of liberal emendation previously indulged in. Clearly, through the increasingly comprehensive textual analyses of Pearce, the Richardsons, and Peck, the state of the two authoritative editions is becoming known and, even if all the substantive variants have not yet been disclosed, serious editors are being warned that a careful collation of the two must be their first consideration.

In the meantime, however, while those three scholars were conducting their investigations and publishing the results, the initial reaction of other editors to the attacks on Bentley was simply to retreat to the non-controversial position of the pre-Bentleian editions. Jacob Tonson III, who had taken over the firm in 1735, brought out several unpretentious editions in 1737, 1738, 1739, and 1741 which were, by and large, slavish reprints of either the 1727 or 1730 texts. And even though Tonson's exclusivism was being challenged by the publication of editions under new imprints (Dublin, 1735; "A Company of Stationers", 1739; Glasgow, 1746), all were based on previous Tonson editions and none took advantage of the recently-exposed textual information. The only editor to profess fidelity was John Hawkey whose Dublin edition of 1747 was, he claimed, free "from the blunders and absurdities ... of the former editions". Hawkey's statement, however, was just as unreliable as those of Bentley. He had indeed undertaken a casual collation and had noted a number of errors and variants but, like all his predecessors, he made the mistake of using a recent edition (the 1738) as his copy-text, thereby perpetuating the progressive corruptions.

In 1749, however, eighty-two years after the first appearance of *Paradise Lost* and seventeen after Bentley's provocation, the foundation laid by Pearce, the Richardsons, and Peck began to be built on and the edifice erected, Dr. Thomas Newton's famous edition *cum notis variorum*, was truly impressive. Not only was it the first variorum edition of an English classic, whose notes – critical and explanatory – would remain standard for the next century, but it was the first definitive text of the poem, based solely on a careful and judicious collation of the two authoritative editions:

> Herein [Newton asserts] the editors of Milton have a considerable advantage over the editors of Shakespear. For the first editions of Shakespear's works being printed from the incorrect copies of the players, there is more room left for conjecture and emendations.... But we who undertake to publish Milton's Paradise Lost are not reduced to that uncertainty; we are not left floting on the wide sea of conjecture, but have a chart and compass

> to steer by; we have an authentic copy to follow in the two editions printed in his own life-time, and have only to correct what may be supposed to be the errors of the press, or mistakes occasioned by the author's blindness. These two editions then ... are proposed as our standard: the variations in each are noted; and we never deviate from them both without assigning, as we think, a substantial reason for it.

For the first time, therefore, all the major variants between the Quarto and Octavo texts are noted and, in several instances, one or the other is defended. At IX.394, for example, Newton chides Bentley for having offered as an emendation a reading ("likest") which, if Bentley had been more diligent, he would have found to be the Quarto reading. At IV.705 Newton offers a very modern-sounding defence of his choice of "shadier": "in the second [edition] we read *In Shadie* bower, but with such a space as is not usual between two words, as if the letter r had occupy'd the room, and by some accident had made no impression." And, finally, Newton's textual perceptiveness, a result no doubt of his scrupulous collation, leads him to a remarkable conclusion, one which many modern editors have been reluctant to accept but which some are now beginning to realize is true: "As to the printing [he states in his note to IX.1092–3] it must be said that of Milton's two editions the first is in general more correct than the second, tho' Mr. Richardson and others have cried up the second as the only genuin and standard edition."

Not merely content to collate the originals, Newton also painstakingly perused nearly all preceding editions. At II.91, II.568, V.455, and at many other places where progressive errors had marred the text, he comments on the absurdity of the emendations. At VI.14, where he notes that in some editions *vanquish'd* had been "absurdly" altered to *vanish'd*, he shows that he was thoroughly acquainted with the 1705–11 editions, and at X.550 he traces a progressive error from the 1695 through to Fenton's 1725 edition. Newton is therefore minutely aware that among previous emendations are only one or two which are acceptable. He would not, he states, feel justified in altering the text to admit Bentley's "swelling" for "smelling" (VII.321), but would do so for "soul" (VII.451): "We are very cautious in admitting any alteration into the text of Milton; but in correcting such mistakes as this we conceive we do no more than Milton himself would have us do." By the same token, Newton admits three further emendations: "metal" for "medal" at III.592, first introduced in 1720; "whether" for "whither" at IV.592, first introduced in 1719; and "too" for "to" at IX.854, introduced by Fenton in 1725. The first two have been almost universally accepted ever since and the third has also found widespread acceptance.

All in all, then, Thomas Newton's edition of *Paradise Lost*, which remained the standard edition for the next half-century, is as modern-looking, in terms of the substantive text, as those of Hughes, Fowler, or Frye. There are errors, of course, for the modern printing techniques (still far from being infallible) were not available to Newton; but his handsome Royal Quartos (in two volumes), soon to become best-sellers on the basis of their *notis cum variorum*, would when examined honestly support the editor's claim that they had been "printed correctly according to Milton's own editions". The text was at last definitive.

It would belabour the issue (and prove unduly monotonous) to reiterate the influence of Richard Bentley on Newton's editorial achievement. Suffice it to say that Bentley's name recurs more often in Newton's notes than any other, and almost always it is accompanied by the corrective comments of either Pearce or Richardson. Bentley's influence, in fact, would continue to be felt, either through Newton's edition or through the (waning) popularity of his own, throughout the eighteenth century and would continue to provoke editors to seek textual fidelity. In 1760, for example, Edward Capell, the well-known Shakespearian bibliophile, dedicated his edition of *Paradise Lost* to Zachary Pearce "for the service [he had] done it, when defac'd ... by an overdaring critick". Textual fidelity – the scientific treatment of the text – was by then becoming, if not reputable, at least acceptable: Capell includes in his textual apparatus not only a list of Quarto-Octavo variants, but a list of internal Quarto variants and quasi-facsimiles of the six Quarto title-pages.

It would not, perhaps, be going too far to suggest that the reaction to Bentley's editorial audacity – to conjectural criticism – was much wider-reaching than I have described. It must be, one feels, more than a mere coincidence that scientific textual criticism, most evident in the treatment of the text of Shakespeare, had its beginnings in the mid-eighteenth century and was promoted by such anti-Bentleian editors as Edward Capell, described by Alice Walker as "the first systematic editor of Shakespeare".[15] In any event, until such a claim is substantiated, one has no hesitation in asserting that, though Bentley's edition of *Paradise Lost* soon lost credibility, its influence – through Pearce, the Richardsons, and Peck – was instrumental in forcing a definitive text for that poem. In other words, an examination of Bentley's edition proves once again that, in literary scholarship as in other areas of human endeavour, an iconoclastic position, defended or denounced, is often the beginning of progress.

NOTES

1 The most important modern studies of Bentley are J. W. Mackail's *Bentley's Milton* (Warton Lecture, XV, London, 1924); William Empson's "Milton and Bentley" (in *Some Versions of Pastoral*, London, 1935); Helen Darbishire's *Milton's "Paradise Lost"* (James Bryce Lecture,

London, 1951); and R. J. White's *Dr. Bentley: A Study in Academic Scarlet* (London, 1965). Bentley's edition of *Paradise Lost* has been reprinted in facsimile by AMS Press, New York, 1974.

2 Empson, *Some Versions of Pastoral* (rpt. Harmondsworth, Mddx., 1966), p. 123.

3 Darbishire, p. 7.

4 Mackail, p. 3.

5 Ibid., p. 15.

6 It is impossible to offer anything more than a precis of the textual history of *Paradise Lost*; for a more detailed discussion see Volumes II and III of Harris Fletcher's facsimile edition of *John Milton's Complete Poetical Works* (Urbana, 1943–8).

7 A complete list of the substantive variants, divided into the three categories mentioned, can be found in my article, "The Text of *Paradise Lost*: A Stemma for the Early Editions," *SB*, 33 (1980), 168–82.

8 For a more detailed discussion of this aspect of the text see the article cited above.

9 John Nichols, *Illustrations of the Literary History of the Eighteenth Century* (1817-18), II, 283.

10 Richard F. Jones, *Lewis Theobald* (New York, 1919), p. 41.

11 Review of Monk's *Life of Bentley* in *The Quarterly Review*, 46 (1831–2), 125.

12 Both J. W. Mackail and Helen Darbishire have made much of the fact that Bentley's copy-text (his copy of the 1720 edition) is available to us for examination. While there indeed exists a copy (Cambridge University Library) which seems to have been owned and marked extensively by Bentley, it is doubtful if this was used as the printer's copy. There is little resemblance between the changes made in that copy and those which finally appear in the 1732 edition. Another copy and a manuscript copy of the commentary must have been used instead.

13 *Philological Inquiries* (1781). Quoted in Jones, op. cit., p. 50.

14 See J. T. Hillhouse, *The Grub-Street Journal* (Durham, N. C., 1928), pp. 84–9.

15 "Edward Capell and his Edition of Shakespeare," *Proceedings of the British Academy*, XLVI (London, 1962), 132.

On Editing Dryden's Virgil

William Frost

Although classic poetry has sometimes been thought to have, and may in fact have, the function of raising its creator or reader above and beyond the contemplation of the merely quotidian, the entirely temporary, the empty vagaries of the passing political scene, it is nevertheless surely incumbent on an editor of such poetry to allow for the possibility that concealed within its text may lie messages which to a contemporary would have arrived with an immediacy not at once apparent to those who came to the same text a couple of centuries later. I am surprised at the editors of the often very useful Longmans Annotated *Poems of Milton* for completely omitting, apropos of *Samson Agonistes* 695–6 –

> ... to the unjust tribunals, under change of times,
> And condemnation of the ungrateful multitude –

for completely omitting any mention of the possibility (seen, for instance, Merritt Hughes) that an allusion is being made to the fate of Charles I's regicides after Charles II's restoration in 1660; and I am grateful to a series of students of Dryden's *Aeneis*, beginning at least as early as that observant peer Lord Holland in 1828,[1] for perceiving that two lines very freely or creatively rendered in Book VI – lines about

> they, who brothers better Claim disown,
> Expel their parents, and usurp the Throne –

pretty unmistakeably allude (there is no expulsion, usurpation, or "Throne" in Virgil at this point) to the recently deceased Queen Mary, who had mounted the throne of her deposed father James II, despite the fact that if James (as his opponents claimed) *had* abdicated, his legitimate successor would have had to be his infant son (Mary's half-brother), also called James. The *Aeneis* came out in 1697; Queen Mary died in 1694; so that it looks as though Dryden were treating her to a posthumous trip to Virgil's Tartarus as an insult to add to the injurious fact that he had never written a funeral ode for her, as he *had* done for her uncle Charles II. But actually – I am grateful to Professor Margaret Boddy for noticing[2] – the person who really sent her to hell was the Jacobite Earl of Lauderdale apparently as early as 1689 (one year after she and William "usurped the Throne"): his translation of Book VI, a manuscript copy of which he sent to James's exiled queen in 1691, and which Dryden had access to in manuscript, contains almost the identical piece of translator's embroidery:

> Here those who Brothers for a crown disown
> Turn out their parents, and usurp the throne ...

Thus it is far from true, what George Watson remarked in a stimulating and otherwise helpful *TLS* article on "Dryden and the Jacobites" in 1973, that Lauderdale's Virgil contains "no political resonances".[3] It does have them; and Dryden took note, and followed suit.

Lauderdale's Virgil, however, had not appeared in print when Dryden's came out in 1697; it remained in manuscript till the earl's heirs published it in the eighteenth century; and consequently the message conveyed by this passage in Book VI first reached the reading public in Dryden's rendition. It then appeared as part of a volume which an alert reader might well have suspected of having contemporary implications. Such a reader could have hardly helped noticing that although at the instance of the publisher Tonson the illustrations of Aeneas (taken over from Ogilby's sumptuous 1668 folio) had been given a "nose-job" to align the hero's profile with that of William III, the Virgil was not dedicated to William, but rather, as George Watson cogently stresses in his article, to three prominent non-Williamites: the *Eclogues* to the Roman Catholic Clifford, the *Georgics* to a nobleman (Chesterfield) who had at first supported William but later refused to take the loyalty oaths to him, and the *Aeneis* to a Catholic sympathizer (Normanby) who was leading the Tory opposition to William's government at the time the Virgil came out. Moreover, in the Dedication of the *Aeneis* Dryden emphasizes the indebtedness of his version to Lauderdale's; and it would have been known that the outlawed Lauderdale had followed James into exile and had recently died in poverty in Paris.

This elaborate 46-page *Aeneis* Dedication is, in fact, a primary piece of evidence for the light in which Dryden saw his Virgilian enterprise in the 1690's. The best approach to it (I think) is by contrast with its source, the document on which it is based, namely the Preface to Jean Regnauld de Segrais' translation of the *Aeneid* into French verse in 1668.

Segrais says relatively little about Virgil's politics, merely noting that the ancient poet was a subject of Augustus Caesar during the *splendeur* of the Roman Empire "in the age the most polite, the most delicate, and the most just that ever existed during the entire duration of the Latin language"[4] and that Augustus was a prince who had loaded the poet with riches and who was himself one of the greatest men whom one could propose as an example for others. Elsewhere Segrais calls the poem a panegyric to Augustus, whose greatest virtue lay in the fine art of government, which he practised successfully for forty years; he says that Virgil modelled Aeneas's character on that of Augustus; and he winds up the long elaborate preface by stating his own aims in these terms: "I have desired to render the *Aeneid* in French as I have conceived he would have rendered it himself, if he had been born a subject of our glorious monarch."[5] In other words, as Virgil was to Augustus, so Segrais will be to Louis XIV, and so the Golden Century of modern France will have been to the Golden Century of ancient Rome.

Set beside Segrais' introductory remarks, Dryden's, in respect to political matters, show a piquant contrast. Alluding explicitly to Segrais' conclusion, Dryden gives *his* aim as follows:

> I may presume to say, and I hope with as much reason as the French translator, that ... I have endeavour'd to make *Virgil* speak such *English* as he wou'd himself have spoken if he had been born in *England*, and in this present Age.[6]

Nothing here about "our glorious Monarch"; instead, "this present Age". As for what sort of an age this present one may be, Dryden leaves us to infer a lot by his detailed discussion of a matter that Segrais entirely omits: the changes in Roman government during Virgil's lifetime, when the ancient republic – and Dryden says that "our great Author [Virgil] ... was still of Republican Principles in his Heart"[7] – when the ancient republic was "subverted" – "subverted" is Dryden's term – and a new autocratic government was established by Augustus Caesar. Instead of Augustus Caesar serving as the model from which Virgil drew (as Segrais thought) the character of Aeneas, Dryden sees Virgil drawing the character of Aeneas – wise, moderate, just, compassionate – as a model to influence the conduct of Augustus Caesar. "I dwell on many things," says Dryden, "which [Segrais] durst not touch: For 'tis dangerous to offend an Arbitrary Master [i.e., Louis XIV]: And every Patron who has the Power of *Augustus* has not his Clemency."[8] We can infer from this, first, that whatever else Dryden may have thought of William III, he did not regard him as "an Arbitrary Master"; and, secondly, that however glorious the regime of the Sun King may have been in the eyes of others or even in his own, Dryden still preferred the mixed and problematic political state of late seventeenth-century England to the well-organized, but monolithic and potentially repressive, condition of affairs in contemporary France.

The biggest difference, then, between the 1668 Preface to Segrais' French *Aeneid* and that of 1697 to Dryden's English one is the very large amount of space given by Dryden to political matters, and the freedom of his comments. To be sure, these comments are presented in the form of Virgil's presumed thoughts about Augustus sixteen hundred years earlier; but with the recognizable profile of William III adorning the pages of the epic in the guise of Aeneas, the epic's hero, it would surely not take very much detective ability on the part of a reader to deduce that when Dryden represented Virgil as considering that "this Conquerour, though of a bad kind, was the very best of it",[9] and as having many similar thoughts on related matters – it would surely not take much detective ability to deduce that a contemporary application might be intended by the translator as enhancing the modern relevance of the translation.

Let me give one final example. In a passage defending

Virgil for committing an anachronism in making the founding of Rome and Carthage contemporary, Segrais says that the rules of poetry were never meant to enslave poets. Closely paralleling Segrais' reasoning on this same point, Dryden suddenly adds a political metaphor all his own; he says that Virgil superseded mere mechanical rules "for the same reason that a monarch may dispense with or suspend his own laws, when he finds it necessary to do so"[10] – a clear allusion to the chief issue at stake when William III was brought over from Holland to oust James: James had suspended previous laws directed against Roman Catholics and dissenters.

I think I have shown how contemporary matters pretty clearly impinge both on the text of Dryden's Virgil and on the extensive prose which he prefixed to it; I now want to add a word about two matters more on the fringes, perhaps, of the edition: Dryden's Notes and Observations at the back of the book, and his – or someone's – assignment of the elaborate illustrations taken over from Ogilby – the assignment of each of these to a specific titled or affluent five-guinea subscriber.

Dryden's Notes and Observations are a part of his Virgil that has had in the past only the most minimal, cursory, or dismissive attention from students and editors of Dryden; even Noyes does almost nothing with them, and Reuben Brower, in his unpublished 1936 dissertation on Dryden's "Use and Criticism of Virgil", merely uses them – without much investigation that I can detect – to illustrate his generalization that they vary from "the surprisingly good to the execrably bad". (One notes that he was surprised that any of them were good at all.) Their miscellaneous character (which scholars are sure to find irritating) cannot be denied; but this fact may not make them less valuable as evidence of what Dryden saw in his author.

A point that George Watson makes in his 1973 *TLS* article which I referred to previously is that Dryden's occasional use of "Immortal" in the translation where it doesn't occur in Virgil may arise from his seeing Rome as immortal in a way Virgil wouldn't have and couldn't have – namely, the way in which the Hind is immortal in *The Hind and the Panther*, which begins "A milk-white Hind, immortal and unchang'd ..." Two of Dryden's notes seem to me to bear on this interpretation. The first is his note on the passage about the suicides in Book VI ("The next, in place and punishment, are they / Who prodigally throw their lives away"). Here Dryden's note refers both to Plato and, rather pointedly, to the Italian commentator Fabrini, whose elaborate sixteenth-century edition of Virgil remains a monument both to Fabrini's Catholic allegorization of the poet and to Italian scholarship and criticism linking Virgil and Dante.[11]

Later in the notes we come across the following comment on Dryden's version of a passage describing a ritual sacrifice on Juno's altar: "The translation is infinitely short of Virgil ... for I could not turn the word *enim* into English with any grace ... 'tis of the same nature ... in our words of consecration at the altar."[12] As a Catholic convert, Dryden could hardly not have been aware of the fact that the words of consecration in the Latin mass (*hoc est enim corpus meum*) come across in the English rite as simply "This is my body", the translation from Latin which he alludes to here. Watson's perception of a value this particular translator would have seen in his original is, I think, reinforced by details like these in Dryden's notes.

About the assignment of illustrations to specific patrons I want to make three points: first, it is clear that at least some of the assignments could not have been arbitrary; secondly, in the light of the hypothesis that a mind (whether Dryden's, or his publisher Tonson's, or somebody else's) was at least sometimes operating to assign a specific illustration to a specific patron, some of the illustrations certainly raise questions about whether a specific symbolic appropriateness may not have been intended; and thirdly, once the question of specific appropriateness has been raised, it is hard, in dealing with the 1690's, not to wonder about possible personal or political meanings or messages.

In what I will say, briefly, about these plates I am much indebted to a fellow Dryden-admirer, Professor Steven Zwicker of Washington University, who came to a talk I gave at a Dryden seminar at the MLA in San Francisco last Christmas, and who since that time has been both corresponding and conferring with me about these plates and about the subscriber list. In a letter of last March he makes three points about the plates in general; after Tonson bought them for the Dryden translation they were altered in three ways: (1) Aeneas's nose was hooked to look like William's (as we have seen), (2) the name and crest of an individual subscriber was added below each plate, and (3) a line number was etched onto each plate to make the illustration refer to a specific line or passage in Dryden's version. Obviously these last two changes set up a situation in which something particular about a subscriber or his or her circumstances in life could be coded into the volume.

Perhaps the most obvious example of a plate that could not have been randomly assigned is the fourth illustration of *Aeneid* VIII, showing Venus delivering to Aeneas the new armour just made by Vulcan: at the centre of the plate the hook-nosed hero is said to "gaz[e] with vast delight" at the shield bearing on its surface at least a half-dozen separate martial or heroic illustrations. The inevitable dedicatee of the plate is Sir Godfrey Kneller, "Principall Painter to his Majesty", to whom, of course, Dryden had written his well-known verse epistle only three years earlier. A few other plates the fitness of whose assignment seems almost equally transparent are the *Pastoral* III plate to Dorset (Palaemon judges a singing contest; Dorset was the great arbiter of the Restoration wits); the first *Georgic* II plate to Bowyer (it shows a handsome estate, and Dryden had paid tribute to Bowyer's country place, Denham

Dryden's Virgil, *Aeneid* VIII, fourth plate.

Dryden's Virgil, *Georgic* II, first plate.

Court, where he translated the first *Georgic* and most of *Aeneid* XII); the first and second *Aeneis* plates to Anne and George of Denmark ("rival" court figures, as Professor Zwicker suggests, to William III, who gets no plate anywhere), the second *Aeneid* III plate, showing a priest and an altar, to the Bishop of Durham; the first *Aeneid* V plate, showing Aeneas leaving some women and old men behind in Sicily, to a captain of the Honourable Band of Gentlemen Pensioners; the fifth *Aeneid* VI plate, showing the sibyl striking awe into Charon's heart by flourishing at him the branch Dryden translates as her "Golden Rod", to Sir Fleetwood Sheppard, who had recently been honoured by being made "Gentleman Usher of the Black Rod"; the third *Aeneid* XII plate, showing the hero's wound being treated in his tent, to the physician Thomas Hobbs; and very possibly the first *Aeneid* XII plate (a noble court scene in which Turnus approaches King Latinus to propose a duel) to the Earl of Chesterfield, the dedicatee of the *Georgics*, a personage Dryden clearly wanted to honour, a nobleman of lifelong experience in royal courts, and even possibly a kind of Turnus figure to contrast with Aeneas as William III.

To the foregoing list of ten pretty clearly appropriate plate-assignments let me add two examples more problematic, examples about which neither Professor Zwicker nor I at present feel very secure. The second *Aeneid* X plate is dedicated to a well-known figure in the Dryden family and literary circle: his brother-in-law Sir Robert Howard, who had been associated with Dryden in sponsoring a play by one of Dryden's sons in the 1690's, who had, of course, exchanged public arguments with Dryden about playwriting as early as the 1660's, and whom Dryden respectfully compliments on his classical and philosophic learning both in the Dedication of the *Aeneis* and in the Notes and Observations on Virgil. The plate, a violent battle scene, shows Aeneas attacking a Latin warrior named Cydon, whose "sev'n bold Brethren" are successfully fending off the chieftain; and the line specified refers disapprovingly to Cydon's homosexual paedophilia: he "courted *Clytius* in his beardless Bloom / And sought with lust obscene polluted Joys" – a disapproval so out of harmony with the actual tone of the Latin at this point that it has drawn down on Dryden such epithets as "coarse", "heavy-handed", and even "ham-fisted" from a recent indignant commentator.[13] To an age (the 1980's) surely not much less gossipy than Dryden's own, the association of Cydon and his brothers (their character somewhat blackened by the translator) with Dryden and his brother-in-law in this way is bound to have an odd ring; the note struck does not *seem* honorific, or at least, not as much so as is the case with several other illustrations.

My other example is the Laocoön plate, the second illustration of *Aeneid* II, in which Laocoön is being strangled by the serpents while his two boys lie dead on the ground. It is dedicated to James, Earl of Salisbury. Concerning the Salisburys, here is an extract from *Burke's Peerage*, 100th edition (1953):

> James, fourth Earl of Salisbury, being a convert to the Roman Catholic faith, was presented to the grand jury of Middlesex, immediately before the Revolution of 1688, as a popish recusant, and on the 26th October 1689 the Commons resolved that he and the Earl of Peterborough be impeached for high treason, for departing from their allegiance, and for joining the Church of Rome, but the prosecution was eventually abandoned. Baptized 1666, died 1694, his only son was James fifth Earl of Salisbury, born 1691....

The older Salisbury, one feels, could hardly have viewed the coming to England of William III with any more enthusiasm than Laocoön did the coming to Troy of the Trojan horse; and, like Laocoön, Salisbury was blessed with male issue. Is

Dryden's Virgil, *Aeneid* VI, fifth plate.

Dryden's Virgil, *Aeneid* II, second plate.

the fact that Laocoön was a priest relevant to Salisbury's faith (the illustration shows a corner of an altar at the left)? Are we to take the serpents as representing the House of Commons? It is tempting, at any rate, to suppose that the assignment of this particular plate was the result of a thoughtful intention on somebody's part, and I would guess the somebody wasn't Tonson.

II

I now want to turn from Dryden's Virgil as a lively response to the translator's immediate circumstances in the 1690's and say something about Dryden's Virgil as a version of Virgil; that is, as a version of a body of poetry – about 18,000 lines in Dryden's translation – that had by Dryden's time been finding responsive readers for more than a millenium and a half, and that would go on finding them, as we know, at least down to our own day. What can be said, in short, about Dryden's Virgil as part of the long-term, on-going Virgilian phenomenon, if you will forgive my putting it that way?

Well, from an editor's point of view at least, the fact is that a good deal has been said, that significant lines of investigation have been opened during the past half century, and that certain directions in which further study ought to proceed have been suggestively indicated. The two areas of investigation are, have been, and will be Dryden's version in relation to the Latin original, and Dryden's version in relation to earlier and later translations of the Latin. I will say something about each of these in turn.

Although Dryden occasionally mentions other editors of Virgil – Heinsius, Pontanus, and (as we have seen) Fabrini are examples – he himself says, and recent scholars have agreed, that the edition from which he chiefly worked was what he calls the Delphin Virgil (i.e., The Dauphin's Virgil), the edition done by Ruaeus (Charles de la Rue) for the Dauphin series and brought out in Paris in 1675. Like other Renaissance editions of classical authors, this one supplied its readers not only with a Latin text based on the editor's decisions in respect to the manuscript evidence (in Virgil's case, not a terribly problematic matter), but also with elaborate Latin notes, as well as a running paraphrase (the *interpretatio*) in Latin prose. Dryden's reliance on Ruaeus was discussed, praised, and well illustrated by Professor James McGrath Bottkol in his pioneering article on Dryden's Latin scholarship in *Modern Philology* in 1943,[14] an article valuably supplemented twenty years later by the Norwegian scholar Arvid Løsnes in the book *The Hidden Sense* by Sofie Røstvig and others.[15] Løsnes showed pretty conclusively that it was Ruaeus's second edition, published in Paris in 1682, in Amsterdam in 1690, and in London as early as 1687, that Dryden was using, rather than the first edition of 1675.

At the time Dryden was translating in the 1690's, however, Ruaeus — on which he certainly placed his main reliance — was not the most recent available scholarly edition of Virgil. In 1680, five years after Ruaeus's first edition, there had appeared in Holland the edition of Emmenessius and Pancratius Masvicius, most of which was done by Emmenessius, whose work Masvicius completed after Emmenessius's death. Dryden didn't like either the Dutch as a nation or Dutch commentators as a scholarly group; so it doesn't seem to me surprising that if he knew this edition he never mentions it. But the fact is that at several points in his own Notes and Observations he purveys information not given, as far as I can see, in Ruaeus, but readily available in the commentary of the learned Emmenessius. One other piece of evidence I have come across — possible evidence, I should say — concerns the text of Virgil. In ninety-nine out of a hundred cases, if not in 999 out of a thousand, the seventeenth-century text of Virgil has no significant difference from one a twentieth-century reader might pick up — from the text of the Loeb edition, for example. But differences nevertheless do occur; James Bottkol discusses three or four, and recently an alert graduate assistant of mine has pointed out another, not previously noticed, I think. In a short list of warriors in Book II Virgil describes one hero as *maximus armis* ("very great in arms") in the accepted modern text, but as *maximus annis* ("very great in years") in Ruaeus. Now the curious thing about this situation (it occurred to me when I started examining the evidence) is that Dryden had translated both readings: naming two heroes who "by my side engage", he continues by having Aeneas characterize them as "For Valour one Renown'd, and one for Age" (l. 458). We have here a method of translating practised, as Priscilla Bawcutt has shown in her recent study, by the earliest British Virgil translator, Gavin Douglas, who completed his *Eneados* on July 22, 1513.[16] At least twice when confronted by variant readings in the scholarly editions he used, Douglas incorporates the meaning of both variants in his version.

But the odd thing about the *armis-annis* dilemma in Book II is that Ruaeus doesn't stigmatize it as a dilemma; he has no note on the passage and includes no variant reading. Dryden could have found the reading *armis* in Heinsius, whose edition he tells us he consulted on line 596 of *Aeneid* IV (see his notes on that book); but Heinsius was unannotated. In Emmenessius, on the other hand, Dryden would have found – if he used Emmenessius – not only the now accepted reading, but also a scholarly note comparing it with the reading *annis* and giving grounds for a choice between them. This is just the sort of note, I think, which might well have triggered Dryden's assimilative, Gavin-Douglas-like response.

So much for the text of Virgil; now a word about Dryden as a member of the extensive Virgil-translating fraternity. Serious modern work on this topic began, about the same time as Professor Bottkol's study of Dryden's scholarship, with Helene Maxwell Hooker's 1945 article on Dryden's

Georgics and their English predecessors,[17] and has had further attention since from four energetic investigators: Margaret Boddy of Minnesota in a series of articles,[18] the British scholar L. Proudfoot in a book on Book IV of Dryden's *Aeneis*,[19] and two American graduate students, Anne Ruth King in her 1949 dissertation on Restoration classics-translating with special attention to Dryden's *Aeneis*,[20] and Adams Betty Smith in her 1970 thesis on the influence of Dryden's version on its eighteenth-century successors.[21]

Helene Hooker's article opened up the topic, and adequately showed the complexity of trying to determine, for a given Virgilian poem, just which predecessor translations Dryden was in fact most influenced by. As for Professor Boddy, though one of her articles deals with Sir Charles Sedley's fourth Georgic, her great achievement has been to throw new light on the translator who stood closest, professionally and personally, to Dryden, the Jacobite Earl of Lauderdale, who put Queen Mary in Virgil's hell, and of whose manuscripts and printed editions Professor Boddy has been making a study for many years. She has caused the printed editions of Lauderdale's version to be officially redated, has determined the chronological order of the Lauderdale manuscripts, and has often delicately discriminated the influence of Lauderdale on Dryden from that of Ogilby or some other predecessor. Although her hypothesis about the redating of certain Dryden correspondence – a hypothesis connected with her suggestion that at some points it may have been Dryden influencing Lauderdale rather than vice versa – has been forcefully rebutted by John Barnard[22] and cannot be taken as yet established, nevertheless her contribution to an understanding of Lauderdale's work is certainly unparalleled in our time.

Lauderdale is one of a number of translators to whom intelligent attention is paid in Proudfoot's *Dryden's Aeneid and its Seventeenth Century Predecessors*, much the fullest study of this topic so far published. It supplies good critical essays on nine predecessors, illustrates Dryden-predecessor relations in more than 130 instances, and raises a number of excellent issues about the quality both of Dryden and of the tradition within which he worked. Proudfoot's volume, however, limits itself to a single book of the *Aeneid*, and to only some of the predecessors who did that book; it has many inaccuracies; and it succeeds in giving, designedly or inadvertently, more than one misleading impression. When Proudfoot begins a sentence, for example, with the concessive clause "If Dryden ignored Fanshawe ... it can only be because of" something or other, it is unsafe to assume that, in fact, Dryden did ignore the work of Fanshawe, or that Proudfoot has shown that Dryden did. And when a later scholar, Arvid Løsnes, remarks that "Proudfoot apparently finds" no evidence that Dryden made use of the French translator Segrais, Løsnes is innocently making a very unsafe assumption indeed – namely that this question has been investigated without result. The fact is that it was investigated, and with definite positive results, by Anne Ruth King in her dissertation eleven years before Proudfoot's book and fourteen before Løsnes's article, but unbeknownst, unfortunately, to either man.

Having said so much, however, I must at once add in celebration of Proudfoot that, like Bottkol earlier but much more explicitly, he has come to Dryden's aid on what I regard as a crucial issue, the question why use predecessors at all? Many very dubious assumptions are in circulation concerning this question – the assumption, for example, that Dryden consulted Lauderdale "as often as he felt pressed for time", that he relied on his English predecessors for rhyme words and found himself turning to them more and more as he weariedly reached the last two books of the *Aeneid*, or that (to quote David Wykes) "Dryden mocked Ogilby in *Mac Flecknoe* as a poetaster, but when, in making his own translation, he was stuck for a rhyme or genuinely tired, Ogilby's version was among those from which he stole."[23] As against this sort of assumption, Proudfoot cogently writes in one of the best and truest passages of his book, as follows:

> I do not accept any of these views [that Dryden consulted predecessors to find out Virgil's sense, for lack of time, or to get suggestions for rhyme words]. Dryden wanted to produce the best version possible in living English ... for Heaven's sake do not let us conclude that he was saving time or work. The perpetual consulting and weighing of texts described by Bottkol and documented by Miss Hooker and myself is unimaginably toilsome and slow. I would very cheerfully undertake to translate into verse any text that I know reasonably well faster and with less labour than any man alive, if he were tied to following Dryden's method. I conclude that Dryden's procedure is intelligible only if we presume that he was seeking a definitive version, constantly embodying in his own work what he thought had been well done, and constantly measuring himself against the best version he could find of any given passage.

Three Virgilian translators about whom very little is said in any Dryden studies published so far are the Scot Gavin Douglas, the Frenchman Segrais, and the Italian Caro. Despite some scepticism on the part of Robert Fitzgerald, I think there is evidence that Dryden had looked at Douglas's work, as would be natural, since it was the best *Aeneid* in any language resembling English that had appeared before his own; and I know there is evidence, plenty of it (some of it turned up by Anne Ruth King), that Dryden knew and consulted Segrais' translation as well as Segrais' Preface, on which his own Dedication was based. As for Hannibal Caro, whom Dryden mentions as "scandalously mean" and prosaic in the Dedication of his *Aeneis* but whose work he had earlier called in the Preface to *Sylvae* "the nearest, the most poetical, and the most sonorous of any translation of the *Æneids*" – as for Hannibal Caro, there is clear evidence, beginning with line 41 of Book I, that Dryden knew and consulted his version, a version which (although Dryden may not have had an inkling of this at the time, and indeed, not all the evidence was then in) bids fair to rival Dryden's own as most successful version of the *Aeneid*, in terms of sheer reader acceptance, ever made in any modern language. Caro's version has gone through at least forty-seven separate editions and reprintings between 1581 and 1954, including at least three in the sixteenth century, six in the seventeenth, five in the eighteenth, twenty-one in the nineteenth, and twelve in the twentieth so far; and has come out in at least eight Italian cities, including Venice, Rome, Florence, Turin, Mantua, and Milan.

If the influence of Virgil in French, Italian, and Middle Scots has been underplayed in studies of Dryden's predecessors up to now, one predecessor whose influence has not been neglected is of course Lauderdale, about whom critics of Dryden from Mark Van Doren to the present have had a good deal to say. Proudfoot, who cites Van Doren and who knows Hooker's work, takes the Lauderdale-Dryden relationship as "nowadays established and generally known", and even talks about charges of plagiarism against Dryden.[24] While not wishing to underrate the Jacobite earl's importance, I think, however, it only fair to Dryden to say that the relationship does not obtain consistently over all parts of Virgil's poetry. Whatever is the case in the *Aeneid*, in the *Georgics* Helene Hooker long ago showed that Thomas May was just as important a predecessor as Lauderdale; and in the *Eclogues*, the first work of Virgil's Dryden undertook, my own investigation has made it clear that Lauderdale was about the fifth or sixth most influential previous translator of the several whom Dryden consulted.

So much for Dryden's relation to earlier versions. As for the fate of Dryden's version after its own appearance, I have already mentioned Adams Betty Smith's very sound study of its influence on its eighteenth-century successors. Instead of supplying you with easily compiled bibliography on its subsequent fate, I will here inject a personal note.

Returning from six weeks in England a year ago last September, I was asked by a customs officer in New York if the trip had been made for business or pleasure. On my answering "both", he asked what was my business in the United Kingdom. Studying a seventeenth-century translation of Virgil, I answered. What do we need a seventeenth-century translation for, he then asked, when we've got Mandelbaum?

Well, the best answer I could come up with on the spur of the moment was the fact that Dryden's *Aeneid* has been reprinted at least half a dozen times in the twentieth century; but I have a better one now. This fall at Santa Barbara I am giving a course in ancient world literature, Homer to Dante, and my original plan was to use Mandelbaum's *Aeneid*, of which I own a paperback copy, on the ground that it would make a difficult classic most easily accessible to the sophomore of today (at any rate, the Californian sophomore of today). When I discovered that Mandelbaum was unfortunately out of print, I then sought Humphries or Day Lewis, only to find that each of these was out of print likewise. I then sought any English translation of the *Aeneid* that was in print, and in paperback, and found that one only was available: Dryden's for $.75. I am about to use it on my return to the coast after this conference, and I think that the enquiring customs officer is now adequately answered, and incidentally the possibility of my receiving a "golden fleece" award from some U.S. Senator or other (for I was travelling on government funds) may have been perhaps somewhat reduced.

III

But why read Virgil at all? I would like to conclude with a few brief words on Dryden and his fellow translators of Virgil into English, regarded from the point of view of this ultimate question. The first witness I want to call is a thorough anti-Virgilian, the well-known poet and classicist Robert Graves.

"Why Virgil's poems have exercised so great an influence," wrote Graves in 1962, "is, paradoxically, because he was a renegade to the true Muse. His pliability; his subservience; his narrowness; his denial of that stubborn imaginative freedom which the true poets who preceded him had prized; his perfect lack of originality, courage, humour, or even animal spirits: these were the negative qualities which first commended him to government circles, and have kept him in favour ever since."[25]

Let us test these generalizations by the character and circumstances of those who translated Virgil in the British Isles during the two centuries from Gavin Douglas's *Eneados* in 1513 to Dryden's Virgil in 1697. These translators, it came rather as a surprise to me to discover, numbered no fewer than fifty, including Dryden and Douglas and excluding Spenser (who translated only from the Virgilian appendix) and Marlowe (who scattered only snatches of Virgil translation throughout his *Tragedy of Dido*). Six of the fifty remain anonymous and unidentified; the forty-four others range from forgotten figures like Charles Hoole, whose 1665 *Georgicks* in Latin and English was once owned by Lincoln's Inn Library but seems to have disappeared since they sold their unique copy; through moderately well-known verse translators like Sandys, famous for his Ovid, or May, the translator and continuator of Lucan; to poets any student of the period will be sure to have come across, like Surrey, Jonson, Crashaw, Vaughan, Waller, Howard, Cowley, Denham, Dryden, and Addison. The amount of Virgil they translated ranged from brief extracts like the passage of *Aeneid* Book IV Jonson included in his *Poetaster*; through complete works like Douglas's *Aeneid* or May's *Georgics*; to the complete Virgils

– *Eclogues*, *Georgics*, and *Aeneid* – achieved during these two centuries only by Ogilby, Lauderdale, and Dryden.

What drew these particular poets or versifiers (all the translations except one or two were in verse) to Virgil, of all authors? "When Virgil's *Aeneid* emerged from centuries of allegorical interpretation, which still informs ... Gavin Douglas's *Eneados*", writes T. W. Harrison, "it was subjected to more and more political specialization. The hidden general truths and sentences become specific moral and political lessons for seventeenth-century England, especially for the years of the Civil War, the Protectorate, and the Restoration."[26] To this I would add, for sixteenth-century England, as well. Consider the following evidence.

The forty-four Virgil translators whose names are known turn out on examination to include at least four privy councillors (Fanshawe, Howard, Lauderdale, and Mulgrave); at least four M.P.s (Wrothe, Waller, Lewkenor, and Addison) as well as one Irish M.P.'s son (Stanyhurst); one monk (temporarily) – Stapylton; five priests, clergymen, or preachers (Stanyhurst, Brinsley, Bidle, Milbourne, and Sacheverell); at least one schoolmaster (Vicars); and something like a dozen who took stands on matters of public controversy. One of the latter may have been Phaer, whose dedication of his *Aeneid* to Queen Mary Tudor has been suspected of being tendentious; among the others at least four wrote controversial religious works; one (Wrothe) moved in Parliament to impeach Charles I; another (Harrington) argued publicly during the interregnum for a republic; a third (Boys) petitioned in 1660 for a free parliament; a fourth (Duke) was the author of lampoons against one or two informers in the Popish-Plot affair; a fifth (Tate) wrote most of *Absalom and Achitophel, Part II*; and a sixth (Sacheverell) preached the sermon that inspired Defoe's satire *The Shortest Way with the Dissenters*. With such feisty tendencies evidently characteristic of at least some of the group, it is no surprise to find that at one time or another more than a few of the Virgilians found themselves either in hot water or in reasonably close proximity to it. Douglas was ousted from his bishopric while visiting the English court; Brinsley was persecuted by the orders of a different and later bishop; Jonson was jailed for a lively bit of anti-Scottish dialogue, unpleasing to James I, in *Eastward Hoe*; Bidle was often imprisoned, was once exiled to the Scilly Isles, had his books condemned to be burnt, and finally died in jail (there was some doubt whether he believed in the divinity of the Holy Ghost, third person of the Trinity); Waller, as every one knows, was imprisoned, fined, and exiled for his part in a plot to hand London over to the royalists during the period of the Civil Wars; Cowley prepared his poetry for publication while in jail as a suspected spy; Crashaw died self-exiled in Italy; Boys, after submitting his petition for a free parliament, had to hide out to escape imprisonment; Harrington was sent to the Tower of London in 1661; Fanshawe was removed from his ambassadorship in Lisbon for taking too much initiative in negotiating treaties; Caryll (uncle of the *Rape-of-the-Lock* Caryll) was briefly jailed during the Popish-Plot hysteria; I have already referred to the outlawed Lauderdale's death in Paris; Sacheverell was impeached, convicted, and forbidden to preach for three years; and Tate lost his laureateship when George I came in, and later died impoverished in the Mint, that refuge of debtors. The inventor of blank verse and translator of two books of the *Aeneid*, Surrey, was eventually beheaded; Godolphin, one of the best translators of *Aeneid* IV, lost his life while on active service at the Battle of Shagford in the Civil Wars; and Stafford, one of the *Eclogue* translators whose work clearly influenced Dryden's, was the son of Viscount Stafford, the most prominent victim of the Popish Plot.

Political, or philosophical, or ideological involvement, including a warm sense of commitment to public concerns, seems to be a common characteristic among many of these translators, who included Thomas May, the historian of the Long Parliament; James Harrington, the political theorist who deeply influenced the founders of the American constitution; and John Denham, the manuscript of whose Virgil, in its earliest state, was preserved in the common place book of a close Denham connection who married in 1638 a future parliamentary general, governor of Nottingham, and regicide. I like to think of the positive contributions some of this group were led to make by the intensity of their concern: May's contribution to history; Harrington's authorship of *Oceana*; or Denham's sponsorship, once he got into power after the Restoration, of the early career of Sir Christopher Wren. Thinking of men like these, it seems to me somehow unlikely that they were drawn to translate the *Aeneid, Georgics*, or *Eclogues* because they sensed in that Latin poetry its author's pliability, subservience, narrowness, denial of imaginative freedom, or lack of originality, courage, humour, or animal spirits. Something like the very opposite of these qualities, I suspect, may have been what these translators thought they saw in their original.

Among this group, it is hardly necessary to add, Dryden was in many respects typical or even prototypical. A lover of Virgil – as can be amply proved from his own writings in prose, in verse, and for the stage – a lover of Virgil from his earliest days, Dryden also, all his life, was, or tried to be, the spokesman for his own time and place, celebrating successively the rules in England of Cromwell, Charles II, and James II, and defending with vigorous satire (his best writing) a tiny imperilled ideological minority from hysterical outbursts of dangerous popular xenophobia comparable to McCarthyism, or worse, in the twentieth century. Having himself joined that tiny minority late in his career, and having seen that career itself imperilled by the sudden discontinuities of a new regime, he remained in London, still a spokesman for his age if also, as always, in some ways a hostile critic of it, and continued to be the centre and great exemplar of a group whom he himself had been recruiting for more than a decade, the translators and revitalizers of the classical tradition. In all this I think he would have been proud to be seen as the heir of such a numerous and rambunctious body of predecessors. In such a tradition, I think, glorious John, as Walter Scott called him, might well have gloried.

NOTES

1 See Alan Roper, "A Critic's Apology for Editing Dryden's *The History of the League*", in J. Max Patrick and Alan Roper, *The Editor as Critic and the Critic as Editor* (Los Angeles: William Andrews Clark Memorial Library, 1973), pp. 49–50 and 68.
2 In her "Contemporary Allusions in Lauderdale's *Aeneid*", N&Q, NS 9 (1962), 386–8.
3 Issue of March 16, pp. 301–2.
4 Jean Regnauld de Segrais, *Traduction de l'Eneide de Virgile*, (Paris, 1668), p. 7; my translation.
5 Ibid., p. 65.
6 *Poems of Dryden*, ed. James Kinsley (Oxford: Clarendon Press, 1958), III, 1055.
7 Ibid. III, 1014.
8 Ibid. III, 1020.
9 Ibid. III, 1014.
10 Ibid. III, 1031.
11 George R. Noyes, *Poems of Dryden*, 2nd. ed. (Boston: Houghton Mifflin, 1950), p. 712b.
12 Ibid., p. 714b.
13 T. W. Harrison, "Dryden's *Aeneid*", in Bruce King, *Dryden's Mind and Art* (Edinburgh: Oliver and Boyd, 1969), pp. 164–5.
14 MP, 40 (1942–3), pp. 241–54.
15 *Norwegian Studies in English*, IX (Oslo: Universitetsforlaget).
16 Priscilla Bawcutt, *Gavin Douglas* (Edinburgh: Edinburgh University Press, 1976), p. 124.

17 "Dryden's Georgics and English Predecessors", *HLQ*, 9 (1945), 273–310.

18 "A Manuscript of Lauderdale's 'Georgics' ", *N&Q*, NS 8 (1961), 433; "Contemporary Allusions in Lauderdale's *Aeneid*", *N&Q*, NS 9 (1962), 386–8; "Dryden-Lauderdale Relationships", *PQ*, 42 (1963), 267–72; "The Manuscripts and Printed Editions of Lauderdale's Virgil, and the Connexion with Dryden", *N&Q*, NS 12 (1965), 144–50; "Tonson's 'Loss of Rowe' ", *N&Q*, NS 13 (1966), 213–14; "The Irrenavigable ... Styx", *N&Q*, NS 16 (1969), 253–5; and 'Two Notes on *Absalom and Achitophel*", *N&Q*, NS 18 (1971), 463–6.

19 *Dryden's Aeneid and Its 17th-Century Predecessors* (Manchester: University of Manchester Press, 1960).

20 "Translation from the Classics during the Restoration with Special Attention to Dryden's *Aeneis*", Diss. Cornell 1949.

21 "Dryden's Translation of Virgil and its 18th-Century Successors", Diss. Michigan State 1970.

22 "The Dates of Six Lauderdale Letters", *PQ*, 42 (1963), 396–403.

23 *A Preface to Dryden* (London: Longman, 1977), p. 51. I will add some instances, drawn from the first six books of the *Aeneid*, where problems or surprises occur in connection with the work of the predecessors: I.41, only Dryden and Caro add Electra to Virgil's cast of characters; III.346, Dryden echoes Caro; IV.5, Dryden's "imprinted" (added to Virgil) has ancestors in Douglas, Surrey, *Dido's Death*, Stanyhurst, Segrais, and Harrington; IV.249–50, strong evidence that Dryden knew Douglas; IV.749–50, Douglas a bit closer to Dryden than are Waller, Ogilby, Vicars, and Phaer (who are also similar); IV.839–40, Lauderdale closest among a group including Vicars, Lewkenor, Ogilby, Douglas, and Denham; V.498–500, hard to tell if Vicars or Lauderdale influenced Dryden more; V.841–2, an anaphora, added to Virgil, parallels one in Segrais; V.1045, only Segrais and Dryden use a rhetorical question here; VI.170–3, Dryden expands Virgil's vv. 115–16 with suggestions from Lauderdale, Segrais, and Caro; VI.566–9, Dryden's phrasing is close to Boys and especially to Douglas; VI.982, Dryden's interpretation of the Latin was anticipated by Douglas and Boys.

24 *Dryden's Aeneid*, p. 168.

25 "The Virgil Cult", *Virginia Quarterly Review*, 38 (1962), 14.

26 Harrison, in *Dryden's Mind and Art*, p. 143.

The Philosophy of the Footnote

A.C. Hamilton

I begin by recounting an episode that occurred to me earlier this term in a seminar on Modern Literary Criticism. It illustrates in brief compass some problems of annotation which must be solved if ever we are to gain a "philosophy of the footnote", the absence of which George Watson laments in his *Study of Literature*. "It is remarkable", he writes, "how little formal attention has been paid in any language to the writing of a commentary. There is no philosophy of the footnote, though any editor with experience in establishing a text and writing a commentary upon it will know that the second function is usually more demanding than the first."[1] In my seminar I read aloud Thomas Campion's "When thou must home to shades of under ground" to show how conventions work in the poem. I prefaced my reading – unfortunately, as it turned out – by saying that this is his best-known poem, one very familiar to all students of English literature. Before I could discuss its use of conventions, however, I was asked to gloss one word but I couldn't. Perhaps many will guess the question but I hope not all have the answer:

> When thou must home to shades of under ground,
> And there ariv'd, a newe admired guest,
> The beauteous spirits do ingirt thee round,
> White Iope, blith Hellen, and the rest,
> To heare the stories of thy finisht love
> From that smoothe toong whose musicke hell can move;
>
> Then wilt thou speake of banqueting delights,
> Of masks and revels which sweete youth did make,
> Of Turnies and great challenges of knights,
> And all these triumphes for thy beauties sake:
> When thou hast told these honours done to thee,
> Then tell, O tell, how thou didst murther me.

A student asked me: "Who is Iope?" At that point I wished I smoked. I had a colleague once who took up pipe-smoking so that he could spend five minutes stuffing and relighting his pipe before responding to difficult questions. I should have had an answer to a simple question about a poem "very familiar to all students of English literature" and one I had read many times. I thought desperately: Io, no longer a cow? Iole, whose jealousy led to Hercules's agonizing death? Perhaps short for Antiope? No other name came to mind. Now if I had an editor's cast of mind, I might have responded: "Clearly Campion has mistaken Iope for Iole"; but I don't, so how could I respond except to look the student straight in the eye and counter: "Iope is a well-known 'beauteous spirit' in Greek mythology"? I didn't because I knew my student, and knew that the next question would be: "Why Iope?" Then I would have been in worse difficulty for I knew that any identification of the name in a footnote, if I had been able to recall it, would offer only useless information. Nor did I respond with the lecturer's usual gambit: "That's a very good question and I'm glad you asked. Would you please prepare a brief report on the matter to present to the seminar next day." Instead, I confessed I didn't know but I would find out.

Later that day I checked through Vivian's edition of Campion's *Works*, from which I had been reading, but found only one note to the poem: "As Mr. Bullen points out, this poem is reminiscent of Propertius, ii. 28." So I read that elegy in which the lover pleads to Persephone and Dis that his lady be spared for already so many thousands of beauties are in hell with them, and he names four:

> Vobiscum est Iope, vobiscum candida Tyro,
> Vobiscum Europe, nec proba Pasiphae.

In only the one detail – the beautiful Iope in hell – is Campion's poem in any way reminiscent of Propertius's elegy. Evidently both Bullen and Vivian assumed that once readers recalled these lines in Propertius, they would know who Iope was. With some trepidation, then, I checked Lamson and Smith's *Golden Hind*, the text in which I first read the poem as a student. There was no note at all. In some panic now, I fully expected to find a note that began, "As every schoolboy knows, Iope is ..." I consulted the text I first used as an instructor, *Poetry of the English Renaissance* by Hebel and Hudson, and there I did find a note: "Campion is probably referring to the Iope who was the daughter of Iphicles and one of the wives of Theseus." Then I found that note picked up, as notes all too often are, by the editors of the University of Toronto's *Representative Poetry*: "Iope. One of the wives of Theseus". I was somewhat relieved now, for even a professor of English cannot be expected to know off hand the names of the daughters of Iphicles or the women ravished by Theseus. Yet had I that information at hand to answer my student's question, he would have been sorry he asked. For the real question remains: why would Campion refer to one of the daughters of Iphicles, together with Helen, accompanying the poet's beloved when she enters hell? It is true that, almost alone among Renaissance poets, he knew Propertius well; but since he was a fine classical scholar and accomplished Latinist, we should assume that he had good reason to choose the name.

Yet the identification seemed suspect: to my knowledge, no daughter of Iphicles had ever figured in any poet's imagination. Hence I continued my search and consulted Richard Sylvester's popular *Anchor Anthology of Sixteenth-Century Poetry*. Here I found Vivian's note revised: "Iope: mentioned by Propertius (II, 28, 51), whose poem serves as Campion's source." (Sylvester's note illustrates a common practice of annotators: building on one's predecessors, adding the thickness of one more coral to the coral-reef that fringes the poem.)

At this point I decided to consult Propertius, turning first to his translators because they are expected to gloss extensively for English readers. The most famous rendering is Pound's *Homage to Sextus Propertius*:

> Persephone and Dis, Dis, have mercy upon her,
> There are enough women in hell,
>   quite enough beautiful women,
> Iope, and Tyro, and Pasiphae, and the formal girls of Achaia,
> Death has his tooth in the lot,
>   Avernus lusts for the lot of them.

Of course, he supplies no note, not even when he had to defend his creative translation over what he calls his own "perfectly literal, and by the same token, perfectly lying and 'spiritually' mendacious translation in the *Canzoni*":

Here let thy clemency, Persephone, hold firm,
Do thou, Pluto, bring here no greater harshness ...
With you is Iope, with you the white-gleaming Tyro.

Yet I found a gloss on Iope in Pound's annotators: first, in Ruthven's *Guide to Ezra Pound's "Personae"*: "either Theseus' wife or Aeolus' daughter", a note that was expanded in Brooker's *Student's Guide to the Selected Poems of Ezra Pound*: "either Antiope, wife of Theseus, or the daughter of Aeolus, god of winds". The latter resorts to the annotator's gambit: "The name was probably used by Propertius for metrical convenience." By now it was clear to me that I must turn to Propertius's editors. In the Penguin Classics, I found the fudging gloss I was tempted to offer my student: "Iope, a legendary Greek beauty". (Clearly the editor didn't know who she was.) I consulted the editors in chronological order of twentieth-century editions. In his edition of the *Elegies* in 1931, S. G. Tremenheere yields to the editor's gambit I mentioned earlier: "Of Iope nothing is known. Hence I read 'Iole', daughter of Eurytus, beloved by Hercules." He adds, "one of Cynthia's slaves was so named", a gloss repeated by Palmer Bovie in 1963. In P. J. Enk's edition of 1962, two Iopes are identified: the daughter of Iphicles married to Theseus, according to Plutarch in his *Life of Theseus*; and the daughter of Aeolus and wife of Cepheus. W. A. Camps, in 1967, appends a note to the second Iope: "in the latter case the name, if genuine, seems to be an alternative to Cassiope." I checked North's translation of the *Life of Theseus* (1579) and found "Joppa, the daughter of Iphicles" in a list of Theseus's wives. Plutarch goes on to tell how Theseus's rape of Helen caused all Attica to be filled with war and blood.

The identification of Iope with Cassiopeia was all the information I needed, although I did waste some time by consulting L. P. Wilkinson's article on "Propertius and Campion" in which he notes in passing that Iope is the eponymous heroine of Joppa.[2] Joppa is the port of Palestine from which Jonah embarked on his voyage into the hell of whale's body. After emerging from speculations on what this could signify, I found the identification in a note to the poem in the *Norton Anthology of English Literature*: "Iope: daughter of Aeolus, also known as Cassiopeia".

Yet what is the reader expected to do with such information? Tuck it away so that when the names of the other children of Aeolus – Sisyphus, Athamas, Salmoneus, Alcyone, and Calyce – are encountered, the reader will know that Iope is their sister? One may be confident that not one of the many thousands of students who have used the *Norton Anthology* has ever profited from that note. The name Cassiopeia will be recalled only as the constellation, the five stars of Cassiopeia's Chair. Yet the information in this gloss – and it is typical of glosses that identify allusions – could easily be made helpful. Cassiopeia's arrogance in boasting that she was more beautiful than the Nereids led Poseidon to loose a sea-monster which ravaged her country and which could be appeased only by the sacrifice of her daughter, Andromeda. Clearly she is a fitting companion to Helen whose beauty led to the fall of Troy and to the lover's mistress whose cruelty has led to his death.

The accepted goal of the annotator is memorably formulated by Dr. Johnson in his *Preface to Shakespeare*: "not a single passage in the whole work has appeared to me ... obscure, which I have not endeavoured to illustrate." Following Johnson, George Watson allows the modern commentator three principal activities in clarifying obscurities: first, to explain linguistic difficulties, whether verbal or syntactical; secondly, to explain social, historical, and especially classical allusions; and thirdly, to unravel and expose complexities and errors in the text itself. Most commentators engage also in a fourth activity: to identify literary sources.

In my paper I propose to challenge all four activities on

the grounds that they are based on inadequate critical assumptions about the nature of poetry and the act of reading.

As a corollary to Johnson's claim that the goal of the annotator is to clarify obscurities in the text, Watson adds that "where there is no obscurity ... the editor certainly has no duty, and arguably no right, to add a note at all." In Campion's poem there would be no "obscurity" for Watson in the line, "From that smoothe toong whose musicke hell can move". Nor, apparently, is there any obscurity for the commentators, for none has glossed the line. Yet do all readers appreciate the allusion to Orpheus who moved hell with his music? The allusion is implicit in Propertius's elegy: the lover pleads with Persephone for his mistress as Orpheus pleaded with her for Eurydice. In Campion's poem, the compliment is wryly undercut: Orpheus sang in hell to free his beloved while the poet's mistress only boasts there of her conquests.

Or to consider only one phrase: "blith Hellen". Do modern readers understand why Helen is called "blithe" even though the word itself is not obscure? That adjective has its place in the history of Helen's reputation from Homer to the Renaissance. At the end of the *Iliad*, Helen remains grieving for Hector's death for now she is left friendless in Troy. In the *Odyssey* there is a contented Helen restored to Menelaus. She recounts an earlier moment when she was at least rejoicing, though not blithe: when Odysseus entered Troy in disguise, he slew many Trojans, causing their women to weep while her heart rejoiced. (In Chapman's translation: "I made triumphs for their lives.") A blithe Helen is found in Philostratus: after she and Achilles die, Poseidon raises a new island where they are heard to revel, to sing, and to tell the story of their loves.[3] Yet it is her Renaissance reputation which brings the sinister suggestions of a blithe Helen in hell. That reputation is illustrated by three references in Shakespeare. In praising Rosalind, Orlando says that Nature gave her "Helen's cheek, but not her heart"; in Sonnet 53, even that beauty becomes deceiving: "On Helen's cheek all art of beauty set", which suggests a painted and deceiving sensual beauty; and, in *Troilus and Cressida*, there is a blithe and very silly Helen memorably conveyed in the line: "This love will undo us all. O Cupid, Cupid, Cupid!" Does "blithe Helen", then, deserve a gloss? I only pose the question because my argument at the moment is that seemingly plain words may deserve annotation as much as obscure ones.

Yet even the most zealous annotator – the one determined that no word shall ever escape his glossing – must allow that generations of readers have enjoyed Campion's poem without knowing who Iope was, why the poet says that his mistress's voice can move hell, and why he calls Helen "blithe". Perhaps the information in such glosses would only distract the reader, only interrupt the imaginative response to a poem whose appeal is direct and immediate rather than learned. Perhaps the only information the reader needs to bring to the poem is some awareness of the convention of *La Belle Dame sans Merci*, the underworld queen whose enchanting song causes the death of her mortal lover, the convention that Northrop Frye calls the "informing myth" of the poem, namely, "the sinister witch in hell gloating over the murdered bodies of her lovers".[4] For Campion, that informing myth was supplied by the Petrarchan convention of the mistress, the more-than-mortal woman who enjoys the power of life and death over her lover.

II

Even though Johnson allowed that commentors clarify obscurities, he urges his readers to ignore their work as long as they are caught up by a play's fable or fiction:

> Let him ... who desires to feel the highest pleasure that the drama can give, read every play from the first scene

> to the last, with utter negligence of all his commentators. When his fancy is once on the wing, let it not stoop at correction or explanation.... Let him read on through brightness and obscurity, through integrity and corruption; let him preserve the comprehension of the dialogue and his interest in the fable.... Particular passages are cleared by notes, but the general effect of the work is weakened. The mind is refrigerated by interruption; the thoughts are diverted from the principal subject....

Johnson's recognition that glossing, however necessary, remains an evil sums up an ambiguity present from the beginning.

As the *OED* shows, the words "gloss" and "gloze" have been associated from their earliest use. In the Greek, *glossa* applied to a foreign or other obscure word which required explanation; in English, its extended application to any word in a text which needed interpretation gathered a sinister sense, "a sophistical or disingenuous interpretation". "Glossa", tongue, became conflated with "gloze" whose root, meaning "to gleam" came to suggest deceptive appearance (gloss sb.2 1.b). The connection between glossing and glozing was emphasized in the Christian centuries by the tension between the word and its interpretation, the letter and the gloss. Chaucer's Summoner explains that he teaches the gloss rather than the text of holy writ, and adds as justification: "Glosynge is a glorious thyng, certeyn, / For lettre sleeth, so as we clerkes seyn." For him, then, it is not the spirit that gives life to what the letter kills but the gloss. At one time I thought it was only a pun to observe that the annotator should not set himself up between the reader and the text, forcing the reader to see through a gloss darkly.[5] Yet "gloss" and "glass" share the same root. Such etymological connections remain to haunt annotators. How may they gloss without glozing, or gloss without glossing over. If a gloss seeks to clarify obscurities in a text, the more clear it is, the more it gains the sense of glozing, "to talk smoothly and speciously". Even as a gloss clarifies a text, it veils it by substituting its words and syntax for the poet's, its plain meaning for the poem's obscurities. In the Renaissance, "reveil" was a variant of "reveal"; assimilated to "veil", it meant "unveil". Yet it suggests also, "to veil again". I conclude that a reader may *only* see through a gloss darkly.

Yet glossing has a long and distinguished history. In the classical period and through to the Renaissance, the compiling of *glossai* was a means of preserving learning and transmitting texts to later readers. By the Renaissance a text was recognized as a classic – almost defined as such – because it had accumulated elaborate commentary. Commentary measured its place in tradition and demonstrated its continuing importance. Accordingly, Renaissance editions of Petrarch, for example, show on the page a small island of text surrounded by a sea of commentary. On many pages of Gesualdo's *spositione* of Petrarch – the edition I own is 1541 – the text is crowded out entirely because almost every word deserves an extended gloss. There is something classical in the visual impact of the book with the different type faces, bold for the poet's words and italic for the expositor's, and different types for the different languages. The burden of scholarship that the text sustains proves that the poet belongs to the major tradition of classical letters. Since Virgil's *Eclogues* appeared with elaborate commentaries and Mantuan's *Adolescentia* with full notes by Badius, Spenser had no choice but to publish his *Shepheardes Calender* with the annotations by E. K. Only in this way could his poem achieve the appearance of an "instant" classic. The experiment was so successful in achieving this end that Spenser planned to publish his *Dreames* separately, telling Harvey that the work has "growen by means of the Glosse (running continually in manner of a paraphrase) full as great as my *Calendar*."

Spenser's language suggests a close and creative collaboration between himself and E. K., as though he wrote with the annotator's work in mind. In his Epistle Prefatory to *The Shepheardes Calender*, E. K. tells Harvey that he has added "a certain Glosse or scholion for thexposition of old wordes and harder phrases: which maner of glosing and commenting, well I wote, wil seeme straunge and rare in our tongue: yet for somuch as I knew many excellent and proper devises both in wordes and matter would passe in the speedy course of reading, either as unknowen, or as not marked, and that in this kind, as in other we might be equal to the learned of other nations, I thought good to take the paines upon me." Instead of annotation serving as a means to rapid reading, its usual purpose in seeking to clarify obscurities, it is used by E. K. to interrupt reading. Colin complains,

> I love thilke lasse, (alas why doe I love?)
> And am forlorne, (alas why am I lorne?)

and E. K. comments: "a prety Epanorthosis in these two verses, and withall a Paronomasia or playing with the word".

The English literary Renaissance is a major period of annotation in part because the classical tradition of annotation stimulated poets to annotate their own works.[6] Ben Jonson is the most obvious example of the collaborative endeavour of the creative and critical mind, particularly in his masques. In the dedication to the *Masque of Queens*, he thanks Prince Henry who had heard the poetry of the masque but wanted to "inquire into her beauties and strengths" with his eye. Accordingly, he surrounds the text by marginal glosses: the page becomes a feast to the typographical eye and an emblem of his "endeavours of art". For Jonson, the "beauties and strengths" of his masque are revealed by the glosses which declare the authorities which support his scholarship. The glosses show that he is massively learned; yet the poetry itself could hardly be less obscure:

> The weather is fair, the wind is good;
> Up, Dame, o' your horse of wood;
> Or else tuck up your gray frock,
> And saddle your goat or your green cock,
> And make his bridle a bottom of thread
> To roll up how many miles you have rid.
> Quickly come away,
> For we all stay.
> Nor yet? Nay, then,
> We'll try her again.
>
> The owl is abroad, the bat and the toad,
> And so is the cat-a-mountain;
> The ant and the mole fit both in a hole,
> And frog peeps out o' the fountain;
> The dogs they do bay, and the timbrels play,
> The spindle is now a-turning;
> The moon it is red and the stars are fled,
> But all the sky is a-burning.

For these lines Jonson glosses very learnedly "horse", "goat", "cock", and "spindle", none being an obscure term over which the modern commentator would pause. I note in passing that the poor modern commentator must gloss "cat-a-mountain" as the one creature unfamiliar to modern readers. Following Herford and Simpson, the gloss is usually rendered in one pathetic phrase: "a wild cat", which suggests to Canadian readers, the bobcat or lynx. The term does not invoke the associations brought to mind by earlier readers when Tyndale rendered John's vision of the beast from the sea as "lyke a Cat off the Mountaine".

In so revealing the "beauties and strengths" of his *Masque* through his glosses, Jonson shows what Sidney means in the

Defence of Poetry when he says that the work of the right poet is accomplished only when the reader understands "why and how" the poet makes his images. In Renaissance poetry generally, the conjunction of the creative and critical in the poet includes the reader.

The tradition of a poet glossing his own works extends to the later Renaissance. It is illustrated most notably in Cowley whose glosses to *Davideis* are longer than the poem and often more interesting. The learning he displays is still massive only now there is a new defensiveness as he labours to prove, in the poetry and in the Notes, that the "Divine Science" may engage in a religious, rather than a profane, subject. Beyond the Renaissance, and so beyond my immediate concern, the tradition is mocked in Pope's *Dunciad* although, of course, the text and gloss must still be read together. It is used grudgingly by Gray who added notes for the general reader to the second edition of his *Progress of Poesy*, but also an epigraph from Pindar to the effect that poetry may be understood by the intelligent while the vulgar need interpreters. Such belligerency indicates that Gray believed the scholarship demanded by the Pindaric ode to be out of touch with his age. He was reluctant to allow his Ode to be shown, "unless to the very few", so he told Warton, "that can scan all the measures in Pindar, and say all the *Scholia* by heart". Cowley was less belligerent, saying only that he doubted whether his Pindaric odes "will be understood by most readers; nay, even by very many who are well enough acquainted with the common roads and ordinary tracks of Poesie". That Ben Jonson published his Pindaric ode, "To the Memory of Sir Lucius Cary and Sir H. Morison" without apology or annotation indicates that the audience for which he wrote was able to understand very complex poetry.

For this reason, I suggest, Renaissance poets were generally content to annotate their poems internally, chiefly by using conventions and genres, various kinds of structuring including the numerological, and authorial comment, either directly or through a persona. I don't believe I am using the term "annotation" too loosely when I suggest that Donne usually annotates his own conceits. In the "Canonization", for example:

> Call us what you will, wee are made such by love;
> Call her one, mee another flye,
> We'are Tapers too, and at our owne cost die,
> And wee in us find th'Eagle and the Dove.
> The Phoenix ridle hath more wit
> By us, we two being one, are it.
> So to one neutrall thing both sexes fit,
> Wee dye and rise the same, and prove
> Mysterious by this love.

As various commentators have shown, a very strict logic governs the sequence of comparisons: as flies they are the same, and destroy themselves in burning tapers, as the taper in burning destroys itself. Then Donne adds a new comparison: the lovers complement each other as do the masculine Eagle and the feminine Dove. These two comparisons (fire and bird) are expressed in the riddle of the Phoenix, which first he glosses: "we two being one, are it" and then adds a commentary: "So to one neutrall thing" etc. Renaissance love poetry especially tended to involve the poet as commentator, beginning, for the English tradition, with the *Vita Nuova* in which Dante embeds the poems in prose commentary that describes their occasion and divisions. Inevitably, the beginning of an extended love poem was the *innamoramento*, the moment of falling in love. Hence Donne's poem in *Songs and Sonets* becomes his gloss on this convention:

> And now good morrow to our waking soules.

Since the lovers in bed together are beginning a new day of

loving, he is announcing his *vita nuova*, the new life which he bids his mistress and his readers to celebrate with him. So also with the "Farewell to Love", where the lover's cynicism comments upon the conventional "farewell to love", in which the poet turns to a higher love, as in Petrarch, or still endures his agony, as in Sidney's *Astrophel and Stella*. That the final word is "taile" bears more than a bawdy significance: it notes the end of a tradition of love-poetry.

III

When poetry began to usurp the place of the classics in education, English poets were subject to extended commentary, as in Patrick Hume's *Annotations on Paradise Lost* (1695) in which he traces all the parallels with Scripture and Homer and Virgil. Such commentary was extended almost infinitely by the rise of historical studies and of literary history in the nineteenth century. Modern annotators are heirs of this long and complex tradition. Yet they may receive little guidance from it, although too many are content to do what has been done. There is no "philosophy of the footnote", I suppose, because English studies began late. Most annotation grew out of historical scholarship that flourished in the late nineteenth and the early twentieth century, with the consequence that we inherit critical assumptions that have been out of date for half a century. As the reader's demands change, the glosses supplied earlier may often strike us as absurd. I would defend them on two grounds. First, they served English studies in their day. In *The Shepheardes Calender*, January 63, for example, Colin complains that Rosalind "deignes not my good will". The modern commentator glosses "deignes not" as "approves not" because that is all the information his reader is expected to need. In his 1895 edition of the poem, Herford appends the following note:

> *deignes not*: ... contracted for "condescends not to accept", probably under the influence of Lat. *dignari*, "think worthy", which, however, is used with an object only of the *person*.

His information is, of course, correct: *dignari*, like *dignus*, takes the ablative of respect. Herford comments as he does because at this time philology dominated English studies. In 1891 Churton Collins complained that, for philologists, "English literature began in the valleys of the Punjab and ended at the birth of Chaucer."

My second reason for defending the earlier commentators is that I complain only when they failed to gloss. In his concluding comment to the November eclogue on the death of Dido, E. K. writes:

> Yet death is not to be counted for evil, nor ... as doome of ill desert. For though the trespasse of the first man brought death into the world, as the guerdon of sinne, yet being overcome by the death of one, that dyed for al, it is now made (as Chaucer sayth) the grene path way to lyfe.

Yet Chaucer does not say anywhere that death has become "the grene path way to lyfe". Since both he and Spenser have received massive attention, one would expect a gloss on E. K.'s reference. Yet there is none: not in the extensively annotated editions of the poem by Herford and Renwick; not in the Variorum; and not in Spurgeon's collection of allusions to Chaucer. It is not mentioned in a recent book on E. K. as annotator. I read through the Parson's Tale three times – I never thought I would – because the phrase should come from there. Then I concluded that it must come from the non-Chaucerian works included in the Renaissance editions of Chaucer by Thynne and Speght. I read through that thick, black-letter folio volume in the Scolar facsimile twice without success. I appealed to Derek Brewer who edited the facsimile, but he has only added to my confusion by telling me that in *Toxophilus* Ascham attacks Idleness as the "enemy of vertue, ye drowner of youthe that tarieth in it, and as Chaucer doth say verie well in the Parsons tale, the greene path weye to hel". Evidently Ascham never read through the *Parson's Tale* and never expected his readers to. Failure to gloss E. K.'s and Ascham's reference is just shoddy scholarship. Alas, I have used the phrase in the title of a forthcoming essay on pastoral; so I shall become the latest offender to gloss over that reference.

The one activity of the annotator usually most immune from changing critical assumptions about the nature of poetry is the third listed by Watson, "to unravel and expose complexities and errors in the text itself". Perhaps most textual matters may be decided objectively on the basis of manuscript authority but some do involve critical judgement. I offer an example from Donne, a stanza from "Twicknam Garden", in Grierson's edition:

> 'Twere wholsomer for mee, that winter did
> Benight the glory of this place,
> And that a grave frost did forbid
> These trees to laugh, and mocke mee to my face;
> But that I may not this disgrace
> Indure, nor yet leave loving, Love let mee
> Some senslesse peece of this place bee;
> Make me a mandrake, so I may groane here,
> Or a stone fountaine weeping out my yeare.

The manuscript evidence on whether to read "groane" or "grow" – allow me this point – is inconclusive. Grierson prefers the former as "surely much more in Donne's style than the colourless and pointless 'growe'. It is, too, in closer touch with the next line." Yet Grierson remained of two minds: the mandrake is "most often said to shriek, sometimes to howl, not to groan" and yet "the lover most often groans." Helen Gardner prefers "grow": "the mandrake was not held to groan when *in situ*; it only groaned when it was torn up." In reply to her Theodore Redpath argues for "groan" as "a more exciting word" that links more clearly with the next line, and adds: "Poets cannot be expected to observe the precise limits of scientific truth. On semantic and aesthetic criteria I believe 'groan' is to be preferred."[7] I find here a clash between a scholar who has defended historical scholarship so strongly in her *Business of Criticism* and a literary critic for whom aesthetic criteria are persuasive. Given the critical temper of the age, when the bibliographer Philip Gaskell maintains that "a textual critic is nothing if he is not a literary critic", I believe Redpath's argument will be found more convincing than Gardner's. I am not surprised that A. L. Clements in the Norton Edition reads "groan", as does A. J. Smith in the Penguin Edition.

The second activity of the commentator for Watson is to explain "social, historical and especially classical allusions". To illustrate an error in a text and in a classical allusion, he cites the line in *2 Henry IV* in which the Page remarks:

> Althaea dreamt she was delivered of a firebrand

with Johnson's comment:

> Shakespeare is here mistaken in his Mythology, and has confounded Althea's firebrand with Hecuba's. The firebrand of Althea was real; but Hecuba, when she was big with Paris, dreamed that she was delivered of a firebrand that consumed the kingdom.

There is one law illustrated by the history of annotation:

"once a gloss, always a gloss"; and it has a corollary: any supposed error by a major writer must always be noted.[8] I doubt if more than a few editors have ever failed to include some version of Johnson's gloss, no matter what the audience. It is found in the Signet Classic edition, the Cambridge, the Penguin, the Riverside and the New Arden. Yet the Page's "error" may be a joke, as Cowden Clarke suggested in 1865. Prince Hal wonders whether the Page has profited from Falstaff's company, and when the Page retorts to Bardolph, "Away, you rascally Althaea's dream, away", the Prince asks him to gloss his classical allusion, which he does incorrectly. The Prince's question is answered: so much for the Page's education under Falstaff's direction.

There may be more than a joke involved. Why is Althaea named? The myth would appeal to Shakespeare because it is a simple, powerful drama. Since Meleager's life depends on a firebrand remaining unburned, his mother Althaea keeps it secure; but when she learns that he has killed her brothers, she throws it into the fire. As it burns, his heart is consumed with flames, and he dies. Then she is driven by grief to take her own life. It becomes clear that she preserves her life while she preserves his. Shakespeare uses the myth of Althaea at the crucial turning-point of the *Henry VI* plays, the opening scene of *2 Henry VI* when Henry's act of giving away his lands causes York to rebel:

> Methinks the realms of England, France, and Ireland
> Bear that proportion to my flesh and blood
> As did the fatal brand Althaea burnt
> Unto the prince's heart of Calydon. (I.i.231–6)

To York, Henry is Althaea who has cast the brand into the fire which takes his life. Later, Henry's action contributes to his own death. There is a similar relation between the Prince and Falstaff, which Shakespeare may anticipate in the Page's retort to Bardolph. Falstaff's final words to Hal are:

> My King! My Jove! I speak to thee my heart!

They provoke his brutal rejection:

> I have long dreamt of such a kind of man ...
> But being awak't I do despise my dream.

We next hear of Falstaff in *Henry V* when the Hostess reports that "the king has killed his heart" – news which Pistol repeats: "His heart is fracted and corroborate" – and then she adds that he is dying: "he is so shak'd of a burning". The "error" suggests that Falstaff is Meleager whose burning heart brings his death, and Hal is Althaea who has chosen his brothers, and notably Prince John, over him.

The learned in Shakespeare's audience would know that Hecuba is the correct allusion, and recalling Hecuba's dream of the firebrand in her womb, they would recall one of Falstaff's finest quips about Bardolph's nose, the parting-shot of their exchange when Bardolph tries to be witty: " 'Sblood, I would my face were in your belly!" only to be crushed by Falstaff's reply: "God-a-mercy! so should I be sure to be heartburnt." On hearing "Althaea" and not Hecuba, they would be prepared for Falstaff's later rejection and death.

In his interesting paper on annotating *Paradise Lost*, E. M. W. Tillyard asks a question which involves Watson's second activity of the commentator balanced against the first, that is "to explain linguistic difficulties, whether verbal or syntactical".[9] Tillyard poses the question: which of two passages in Shakespeare's *Troilus and Cressida* is in greater need of annotation: the one where Nestor speaks of the "ruffian Boreas enraging the gentle Thetis", in which Shakespeare has mistaken Thetis for Tethys, the wife of Oceanus; or the one where Ulysses compares Time to "a fashionable host /

That lightly shakes the parting guest by the hand", in which "fashionable" does not carry the modern sense of "smart", as in the cliché "fashionable hostess", but the earlier sense, "adaptable to the changes of fashion". From the way he poses the question, one knows his answer, but no recent editor agrees with him. They are content to point out that Shakespeare has mistaken Thetis for Tethys. Why should this be? Is it the "catching-Homer-nodding" syndrome? "O. K., Shakespeare may be the world's greatest writer but the dum-dum didn't know Thetis from Tethys." Why do editors want to correct a minor piece of Greek mythology at a time when even Apollo needs a gloss?

The irony of this corrective note is that Shakespeare may well be making a scholarly point in a very scholarly play, one which the members of the Inns of Court, to which the play is directed, would have appreciated. In his *Mythologiae*, Comes treats both goddesses in one chapter, weighing one against the other, and concludes that each goddess was the sea, whether we call the sea Thetis or Tethys. For Shakespeare Thetis is the name to be preferred in a play in which one of the central characters is her son, Achilles. Further, Thetis inhabited Shakespeare's imagination, as his reference in *Pericles* to Marina as "Thetis' birth-child" suggests. It also inhabited Spenser's imagination, and probably for the same reason: the marriage of Thetis and Peleus led to the judgement of Paris and the story of Troy.

The concern of editors to correct Shakespeare's "error" about Thetis has allowed readers to miss the fine irony of the moment in *Antony and Cleopatra* when Enobarbus and the others urge Antony not to fight at sea where he must lose. Yet Antony is determined to fight at sea, and as he storms out, he says first to the others, "We'll to our ship", and then to Cleopatra, "Away, my Thetis". Clearly she is the sea, which leads to his downfall. Yet every edition I have checked notes that Thetis is a sea-nymph.

Of course, this annotator's game is not confined to Shakespeare. When Spenser refers to "the marble Pillour, that is pight / Upon the top of Mount Olympus hight", Dodge comments that Sidney also "makes the same, to us almost inconceivable, blunder" of Olympus for Olympia. As a consequence, one may find in annotated editions of both writers the inevitable gloss: Collins, Cook, Shepherd, van Dorsten, Soens (who writes that Sidney confuses Olympus with "Olympias"! he himself confusing Olympia with the wife of Philip II). For Spenser, the error is noted by Roche and also by Hamilton. If a reader knew that Mount Olympus at 9,700 feet is perpetually snow-covered and concluded that the marble pillar must serve as a marker for the grand slalom in skiing, perhaps such a reader would need to be told that the reference was correct, so far as Spenser and Sidney knew. But then the reader should be told also how fitting that Olympic games should be played on Mount Olympus for Spenser locates most kinds of heroic activity on a mountain-top.

Tillyard's suggestion that commentators should gloss words still current but with altered meanings has not been generally accepted. It is easy to justify a gloss on "cat-a-mountain" in Jonson's *Masque of Queens*, even though a short gloss is more misleading than helpful: the word is obsolete and the modern reader won't know what it means. It is also easy to gloss: check the *OED*. It is more difficult to justify a gloss on "senslesse" in "Twicknam Garden" in the line cited earlier:

> let mee
> Some senslesse peece of this place bee

because its rare or obsolete sense, "insensible" (*OED* 2), which it has here, is not far removed from "devoid of sense, stupid" (*OED* 3), its current meaning. Since words change their direct meanings and overtones from year to year, there would be no end to glossing. What words should not be glossed in the opening line of *The Faerie Queene*?

> A gentle knight was pricking on the plaine

Of the nine senses of "gentle", five are said by the OED to be archaic or obsolete. Yet of these obsolete senses, OED 5, "not harsh or irritating to the touch" is a dominant sense now, thanks to the advertising about kitchen soaps which are "so gentle" to the hands. The modern reader misses entirely the cluster of meanings dominant in the sixteenth century: that the "gentle Knight" may be well-born socially, or of honourable birth, or noble, generous, and courteous. Nor does the word bring to the modern reader's mind important associated words, such as "gent", "Gentile" (which had the same spelling), and "gentilesse". The term "knight" carries none of the earlier, precise sense of one devoted to the service of a lady as her attendant or champion (OED 3). If modern readers take "pricking" as a bawdy quibble, as I suspect they do, they will be distracted from the paradox of the knight who spurs his horse at the same time he reins it in. Yet the term in Spenser's poem means "rashness", a sense which the OED does not supply but which any reader may infer from its use in the poem: it describes the Knight when he flees from Una in jealous rage and when he attacks Guyon, Sansloy when he attacks Archimago disguised as the Knight, Mortdant when he leaves Amavia, Pyrocles attacking Guyon, Maleger attacking Arthur, Blandamour attacking Britomart and Ferraugh, Paridell and Geryoneo's Seneschall attacking Arthur, Crudor attacking Calidore, and the two false knights who attack Arthur in Book VI. The term is applied consistently to evil characters, or good characters overcome by evil emotions, with one exception: it describes Britomart when she first appears in Book III riding with Glauce and at the end of the Book when she pursues Ollyphant. By this time the reader should be able to bring to the term some associations that will recognize the explosive violence in Britomart which her chastity controls. As for the term "plaine", no gloss extracted from any dictionary defines the complex meanings it carries in Spenser's language of allegory. Only the poem itself defines that word – as, in fact, it defines the meaning of every word in it – through the relation of allegorical settings and landscapes.

Tillyard cites "stupidly good", in *Paradise Lost* IX when Satan sees Eve among the flowers:

> That space the evil one abstracted stood
> From his own evil, and for the time remained
> Stupidly good, of enmity disarmed,
> Of guile, of hate, of envy, of revenge

as a term which requires the gloss, "dazed" but doesn't get one. He is correct, of course; yet how may an annotator accommodate the gloss suggested by a critic who recognizes the radical ambiguity of words in poetry, such as Cleanth Brooks, who writes:

> "Stupidly good" constitutes the pivot for the whole passage. What does it mean? "To stupify" originally is to astound, to stun. Satan is momentarily "good" from bewilderment. But "stupify" suggests too a kind of torpor, a numbness or Stupor.... But when the Evil one is abstracted from his own evil, he is not only good (as separated from evil), but stupidly so, for he has so thoroughly given himself up to evil that he is now abstracted from part of himself, and can be "good" only in a dazed and stupid manner, having lost his wits, his directing purpose. If, on the other hand, we remember the pleasant rural setting, with its smell of grain and tedded hay, "stupidly good" acknowledges the rural setting, and accommodates Satan to the rustic scene.

Brooks adds to this extended gloss: "I do not believe that I have exhausted the meanings of the phrase – certainly not all the shadings of meaning. But all that I have been able to think of are relevant."[10]

A critical revolution in the history of annotation began when Empson embraced the multiple meanings of words and images in poetry, in opposition to editors who wished to qualify their importance and even their presence. The consequences of his revolution are manifest in Stephen Booth's "analytic commentary" on Shakespeare's *Sonnets* in which he argues for "an unmediated analysis" of a poem, that is, one "that does not try to decide which of a poem's actions should be acknowledged but instead tries to explain the means by which all a poem's improbably sorted actions coexist and cohere within the poem and, for the duration of the poem, within the mind of the reader."[11] Accordingly, he rejects the customary notes which are designed to explain what a poem means or what the poet says because they "usually end up treating the actual words and their sequence as attendant inconveniences of verse. Such notes often begin with 'i.e.' and state the substance of a line in a syntax completely foreign to the one in the poem." In contrast, his glosses attempt to record the effects of the words in the mind of the reader while reading, and hence with all possible meanings, suggestions, overtones, echoes, and possible implications that may "merely cross a reader's mind" (p. xi).

While the fullness and complexity of his commentary prevent me from illustrating even briefly what he says about any sonnet – for he tries to make the reader aware, as he says, "of the multitudinous statements, ideas, ideals, standards, and references that almost every line of the 154 sonnets contains", I will pause on Sonnet 116:

> Let me not to the marriage of true minds
> Admit impediments. Love is not love

Which alters when it alteration finds,
Or bends with the remover to remove.
O no, it is an ever-fixed mark
That looks on tempests and is never shaken;
It is the star to every wand'ring bark,
Whose worth's unknown, although his height be taken.
Love's not time's fool, though rosy lips and cheeks
Within his bending sickle's compass come.
Love alters not with his brief hours and weeks,
But bears it out ev'n to the edge of doom.
  If this be error and upon me proved,
  I never writ, nor no man ever loved.

His annotations to this sonnet show his readiness to accept alternative meanings. For example, for "with" in line 4, Redpath glosses "*not* in company with" but Booth glosses: "(1) in the company of, along with; (2) like". He does so because "bends" means not only "turns aside" but also "applies all one's energy, attention, and concern to one object", "stooping", and "submission". On the other hand, Booth is quite ready to gloss "bark" as "boat", which must be a first, but now probably necessary. My colleague George Whalley, in his Inaugural Cappon Lecture, observed that one of his students took "wand'ring bark" to refer to a stray dog. Ever since, I pause to look for puzzled expressions when I have occasion to cite the lines in *Lycidas*: "It was that fatal and perfidious bark ... / That sunk so low that sacred head of thine."

Even while Booth develops the elaborate complexity of meanings in lines 5–7, for example, he admits that the lines "do not demand any explanation". What interests him finally is not the meaning of the words but their effect on the reader. He admits some validity to the charge that his analytic commentary reverses all other commentary, for his notes do not try to clarify the sonnets but instead transform lines "that are simple and clear into something complex and obscure". Yet he wants to reject that charge because his purpose is to explain the power of the sonnets in all their simplicity upon the mind of the reader. Booth's arguments – if they are persuasive, but it is too early to tell – should help free commentary from its traditional preoccupation, to clarify verbal and syntactical obscurities in a text.

For there are other matters that should concern a commentator. One is the rhythm of a line of poetry. Tillyard urges that annotators comment on the rhythm of a line when modern pronunciation of a word murders the line with false accents. He cites the line in *Hamlet* in which the French derivation of "commendable" led the Elizabethans to stress its first and third syllables. He reads:

> Tis sweet and com-/menda-/ble in your nature, Hamlet.

He may be right but I prefer to read the line with the normal four stresses:

> Tis swe/et and commen/dable in your na/ture, Ham/let.

Yet the attention Tillyard gives to rhythm is correct even where there is no change in pronunciation. In the opening lines of *Paradise Lost*, for example, "all our woe" may deserve to be glossed as the key phrase in the poem, with a learned note pointing out that all evil follows from original sin.[12] Once the lines are read aloud, however, any note becomes superfluous:

> Of man's first disobedience, and the fruit
> Of that forbidden tree, whose mortal taste
> Brought death into the world, and all our woe ...

The almost equal stress upon the three final words, enforced by their echoing vowels, registers their full import.

Rhythm may be a key to understanding when no amount of information in any gloss will help. Recently I was confronted by the problem of understanding certain lines in *The Shepheardes Calender*. They occur in November, the key eclogue in the poem because here for the first time Colin sings his own song, no longer paralyzed in self-regarding lament. They occur at the key point in the eclogue where Colin's apocalyptic vision of the resurrected Dido is about to break through the zodiac which has encircled all his endeavours until this point:

> O trustlesse state of earthly things, and slipper hope
> Of mortal men, that swincke and sweate for nought,
> And shooting wide, doe misse the marked scope:
> Now have I learnd (a lesson derely bought)
> That nys on earth assuraunce to be sought:
> For what might be in earthlie mould,
> That did her buried body hould,
> O heavie herse,
> Yet saw I on the beare when it was brought
> O carefull verse.

Here the sight of the dead Dido forces Colin to realize, as it forces Milton to realize at just the same point in his elegy to Lycidas, that the dead body he sees is not the person herself. That recognition brings the dramatic reversal and the vision of the resurrected Dido in a heavenly pastoral landscape, walking in "fieldes ay fresh, the grasse ay greene".

How should one read these final lines? and especially, what stress does one give "That"? Is it a conjunction or a demonstrative adjective or pronoun? Renwick reads: "her body (now buried) held whatever of virtue, etc. the human body could enclose"; but then his paraphrase concludes lamely, "yet I saw the day when it was brought on the bier." The

Variorum Editors read: "whatever there is in earthly mould which her body (now buried) possessed"; but they also conclude lamely, changing "Yet" to "that": "that I saw when it was brought on the bier". Or may one read: "Nothing is sure on earth, for even one whose earthly body held the best that might be of earthly value, 'yet saw I', i.e. even her I saw on the bier." I can only suggest that the uncertainty in reading these lines aloud registers the poet's uncertain mood as he hovers between despair at Dido's death and joy at her coming resurrection.

Interest in poetic rhythm has been renewed recently by Stanley Fish's claim that meanings arise from the temporal flow of the reading experience at each stage of comprehension. Premature perceptual closure at the end of a line establishes an independent meaning which is not cancelled by lines that follow. He illustrates his claim by citing the lines from *Lycidas* which describe the consequences of Lycidas's death:

> The willows and the hazel copses green
> Shall now no more be seen,
> Fanning their joyous leaves to thy soft lays.[13]

At the end of the second line, according to Fish, the reader assumes that the willows and hazel copses will not be seen by anyone for they will die with Lycidas. Then the third line adds to this meaning: the willows and hazel copses will be seen but not by Lycidas. In a dismissive response, Meyer Abrams has applied premature perceptual closures to the concluding lines of Milton's poem:

> At last he rose, and twitch'd. His mantle blew.
> Tomorrow to fresh Woods, and Pastures new.[14]

For me, the effectiveness of this parody enforces the importance of Fish's insight. Accordingly, I defend the aural effect of poetry as a proper concern for the annotator.

Another area of concern neglected by the annotator is the visual element in poetry, its use particularly of icons and emblems. In Sidney's *Astrophel and Stella*, the second sonnet describes Astrophel's initiation into love through an icon, "the mine of time":

Not at first sight, nor with a dribbed shot
  Love gave the wound, which while I breathe will bleed:
  But knowne worth did in mine of time proceed,
Till by degrees it had full conquest got.
I saw and like, I liked but loved not,
  I loved, but straight did not what Love decreed:
  At length to Love's decrees, I forc'd, agreed,
Yet with repining at so partiall lot.
  Now even that footstep of lost libertie
Is gone, and now like slave-borne Muscovite,
I call it praise to suffer Tyrannie;
And now employ the remnant of my wit,
  To make my selfe beleeve, that all is well,
  While with a feeling skill I paint my hell.

The concluding sonnet defines his state of loving through the emblem of the sealed furnace:

When sorrow (using mine owne fier's might)
  Melts downe his lead into my boyling brest,
  Through that darke fornace to my hart opprest,
There shines a joy from thee my only light;
But soone as thought of thee breeds my delight,
  And my yong soule flutters to thee his nest,
  Most rude dispaire my daily unbidden guest,
Clips streight my wings, streight wraps me in his night,
  And makes me then bow downe my head, and say,
Ah what doth Phoebus' gold that wretch availe,

Whom iron doores do keepe from use of day?
So strangely (alas) thy works in me prevaile,
 That in my woes for thee thou art my joy,
 And in my joyes for thee my only annoy.

My point is simple and so I shall make it brief. Even though "mine of Time" in Sonnet 2 is the complex out of which the sonnet sequence evolves, annotators have done nothing more with it than repeat the gloss first given by Pollard: "a metaphor from mining operations in sieges". Ringler embroiders slightly, "a tunnel dug in siege operations"; Hebel and Hudson are more cautious, "used in a military sense"; but no one adds anything, even though, in the extended iconology of Time, Time as Pioneer, Underminer, or Sapper seems unique to Sidney. I speak in an aggrieved tone. When I was asked once to lecture on "Sidney and Time", I expected commentators to have remarked on the phrase.[15] If they don't, who will? Who else cares about a poem's literal level of meaning? Or rather, to use the traditional metaphor: who but the annotator is concerned with the literal and tropological levels of meaning, that is, the poem in itself and in relation to the reader? Certainly not the editor whose business is to establish the text. Not the scholar whose commentary treats allegorical levels of significance. Not the literary critic whose concern is with the anagogic level of significance, that is, with the larger literary contexts through which the poem is possessed.

"Mine of time" indicates an explosive force of love that comes from below, a lust in the loins rather than emotion in the heart, a force deeply within the lover, part of him and apart from his lady. Spenser's comparable image is the rankling wound, not simply infected but rabid and possibly syphilitic; but Sidney's image better expresses the internal violence that destroys man's wholeness or holiness. Since this image is realized in the later sonnets, one might expect commentators to consider it. Instead, they expand Mona Wilson's gloss on

"Muscovite" because such information is so easy to assemble and at great length; because the information is factual – just how did the Elizabethans regard the Russians? – and generally educational; and because it is so entirely irrelevant to the text that the note becomes independent – hence Katherine Duncan-Jones addition that Sidney is referring to Slavs, not Russians.

If Sidney studies had flourished earlier in this century, a brisk controversy would have developed in the learned journals: did Sidney really despise the Russians? Was his view shared by the age? Did he know any Russians? Or is he referring to Slavs, not Russians? If Sidney studies flourish in the future when we read poetry on the computer, we may be able to get all the facts by punching out "Muscovite".

On Sonnet 108 I may speak even more briefly. Not a single commentator has glossed "that dark furnace" although the sealed fiery furnace of the lover's heart is an important Renaissance emblem of unsatisfied desire; it is the Biblical image of fallen, unredeemed man suffering under God's wrath, as in Psalm 21:9: "Thou shalt make them as a fiery furnace in the time of thine anger"; and it defines, fully and finally, Astrophel's state as the "lover of the star", one enclosed in darkness gazing up at the heavenly light. I do not believe that the complex tradition behind Sidney's emblem is so well-known to all readers that no gloss is needed. I believe rather that annotators haven't done their job because they have been concerned with the easy way out, with the conceptual approaches to verbal elements in a poem rather than to the more difficult visual elements.

Any "philosophy of the footnote" that I would endorse in conclusion is implicit in my earlier remarks. Annotators need to become aware of the critical assumptions that determine what they choose to gloss, and then choose to say or not say. Only a very little critical sophistication would abort the all-too-usual compiling of miscellaneous information in which anything goes if only it seems somehow relevant or sufficiently learned. No facts should be brought to a poem – historical background, identification of allusions, or ideas – without demonstrating their direct relevance to the reader's understanding of the text. All annotators should become aware, as indeed some have, of what has happened in literary criticism in the past fifty years. Annotation of *Paradise Lost* remained largely unchanged for the 300 years between Patrick Hume's *Annotations* in 1695 and Merritt Hughes's edition in 1957. For example, both paraphrase the lines in Book IX where Milton relates his epic to Homer's and Virgil's. Alastair Fowler's edition in 1968 marks a shift: instead of involving readers in classical learning, as earlier annotators had done, he involves them in the poem. Thus he doesn't gloss Achilles, as does Warton: "the wrath of Achilles [was] celebrated by Homer in the *Iliad*"; instead he explains why Achilles was called "stern" and goes on to contrast the Messiah who "more heroically, is not implacable in his anger. He issued his sole commandment 'sternly'; but when it is disobeyed, he works for reconciliation." I cite this gloss not to defend it but to mark a shift in critical emphasis from the poem in relation to the reader. That shift results from a shift in critical assumptions in modern criticism about the nature of poetry, from asking for "truth of coherence" rather than "truth of correspondence". Fowler helps the reader possess the poem by relating its parts, and is not content simply to accumulate knowledge about it. He is not alone, of course: among the annotators I have cited earlier, Stephen Orgel remarks in his edition of Jonson's masques: "annotation is most helpful not when it identifies or defines details but when it clarifies the context of the details."

Only the annotators make it their business to mediate directly between the poem and its readers. leading them to the poem by removing whatever stands in the way of their possessing it. Only they lead them to the words in the poem, to the words primarily and not to their "reference" or "thought" or "ideational content" (an ugly phrase but well deserved). For all his delightful faults as an annotator, E. K. does appreciate what he terms "the brightnesse of brave and glorious words" in Spenser's poem. It is the business of the annotator alone – never trust the scholar or critic! – to point to the poet's words, the "simple, sensuous, and passionate" words in their imaginative directness and in their fittingness in their context. I recall the abyss that once opened up for me when I asked a class to identify quotations in a Shakespeare examination. I cited the exclamation by the Prince of Arragon when he opened Portia's silver casket:

> What's here? the portrait of a blinking idiot!

One student responded: "Richard II looking at himself in the mirror during the Deposition Scene". Clearly *I* had flunked the course, not the student; but he might have had a chance, in spite of his instructor, if the annotator of our text had noted the decorum of words in a play. It is often said of scholar X or critic Y that it is difficult to imagine them ever reading poetry, and impossible to imagine them reading poetry for pleasure. Such a remark is unfair because they inhabit their own worlds of Christian Humanism, Romanticism, Freudianism, Marxism, etc. In contrast, the annotator's only world is the world of the poem.

Since annotators are concerned with the poetic nature of words, with qualities, then, far beyond critical exegesis or historical background ever to clarify, their *primary* goal is not to remove obscurities. That only invites the reader's passivity, saying, in effect, "this poem may be difficult so let me allow you to 'speed-read' it by putting it in my own words and syntax." That kills any active, imaginative response. The term "obscurities belongs to ordinary discourse where we may never understand what someone means by what he says, not to major poetry where the only obscurity lies in the reader. Yet annotation should not offer what the reader may think he needs but what the poem demands. If annotators do their proper business, they will fashion the ideal reader for the poem under scrutiny, one who may recreate and so possess it.

Finally, the annotator should never forget Johnson' remark that notes are necessary evils, and always ask of each one: "Will this do much more harm than good?" Hence I conclude by endorsing Johnson' claim that the reader should first ignore the work of the commentator:

> Parts are not to be examined till the whole has been surveyed; there is a kind of intellectual remoteness necessary for the comprhension of any great work in its full design and its true proportions; a close approach shews the smaller niceties, but the beauty of the whole is discerned no longer.

In fact, my whole address may be summed up as a gloss to his claim: the annotator should seek only to show "any great work in its full design and its true proportions".

NOTES

1 George Watson, *The Study of Literature* (London, 1969), pp. 132-3. This Conference has made notable efforts to achieve a philosophy of the footnote: see W. J. B. Owen, "Annotating Wordsworth", in *Editing Texts of the Romantic Period*, ed. John D. Baird (Toronto, 1972), pp. 47-72; and John Carroll, "On Annotating *Clarissa*", in *Editing Eighteenth Century Novels*, ed. G. E. Bentley, Jr. (Toronto, 1973), pp. 49-66. See also Arthur Friedman, "Principles of Historical Annotation in Critical Editions of Modern Texts", *English Institute Annual 1941*, pp. 115-28.

2 *London Magazine*, 7 (1967), 56-65. Only later did I learn that Wilkinson's

note is found in H. E. Butler and E. A. Barber, eds., *The Elegies of Propertius* (Oxford, 1933), and that all the information I needed was given in the 1912 Loeb edition.

3 I owe this reference to John Pollard, *Helen of Troy* (London, 1965), p. 181.

4 Northrop Frye, *The Educated Imagination* (Bloomington, 1964), p. 52. Cf. *Fables of Identity* (New York, 1963), p. 96.

5 "On annotating Spenser's *Faerie Queene*: a new approach to the poem", in *Contemporary Thought on Edmund Spenser*, ed. Richard C. Frushell and Bernard J. Vondersmith (Carbondale, 1975), pp. 41-60.

6 There is a place for a study of the annotations by Renaissance poets of their own works through glosses, marginal glosses, dedicatory poems, and epistles designed to teach the reader how to read their works. The tradition illustrated, for example, in Chapman's annotations to *The Shadow of Night* continues through Coleridge's marginal glosses to the second edition of *The Rime of the Ancient Mariner* through to T. S. Eliot's glosses to *The Waste Land.* An excellent introduction to one part of such a study is found in Lawrence Lipkins, "The Marginal Gloss", *Critical Inquiry*, 3 (1977), 609-55. In *Criticism in the Wilderness* (New Haven, 1980), Geoffrey H. Hartman notes that recently forms of critical commentary have emerged "that challenge the dichotomy of reading and writing." He cites Nabokov's *Pale Fire*, the essays of Borges, Harold Bloom's *The Anxiety of Influence*, and Jacques Derrida's *Glas* as examples of "literary texts in their own right as well as commentary" (p. 20).

7 "Some textual problems in Donne's *Songs and Sonets*", *Essays and Studies 1979*, p. 78.

8 This law is illustrated by John C. Meagher, "Vanity, Lear's feather, and the pathology of editorial annotation", in *Shakespeare 1971*, ed. Clifford Leech and J. M. R. Margeson (Toronto, 1972). Kent's assault on Oswald because he "takes Vanitie the puppets part, against the Royaltie of her father" is glossed by Johnson: "alluding to the old Moralities ... in which Vanity ... and other vices were personified". As Meagher notes, Johnson's comment has been repeated by virtually every subsequent editor even though there are no extant moralities in which Lady Vanity appears. As he notes, "the gloss remains conjectural, misleading, and in any event unilluminating cross-reference to the moralities" (p. 246). Yet two years later the same gloss appears in the Riverside Shakespeare, and so it will endure until there is some philosophy of the footnote

or editors are fined for including it.

9 "On annotating *Paradise Lost*, Books IX and X", *JEGP* 60 (1961), 808–16.

10 "Milton and the New Criticism", in *A Shaping Joy: Studies in the Writer's Craft* (New York, 1971), pp. 14–15. Clearly the New Critical method has become a victim of its own success. The same misfortune overcame historical criticism. Rosalind L. Colie allows that the four-line medieval lyric, "O western wind, when wilt thou blow?", "looks frightfully simple; but such reduced production is in fact very sophisticated, and depends upon the charged meaning of endless love-accounts and fantasies in chivalric romance and other courtly lyrics" ("Literature and History", in *Relations of Literary Study*, ed. James Thorpe, New York, 1967, p. 12).

11 *Shakespeare's Sonnets* (New Haven, 1977), p. 515.

12 Isabel MacCaffrey, *"Paradise Lost" as "Myth"* (Cambridge, Mass., 1959), p. 84. There is an excellent note on the phrase by David Daiches, "The opening of *Paradise Lost*", in *The Living Milton*, ed. Frank Kermode (London, 1960), p. 58.

13 "Interpreting the Variorum", *Critical Inquiry*, 2 (1976), 465–85.

14 "How to do things with texts", *Partisan Review*, 46 (1979), 578.

15 I record my struggles with the phrase in "The 'mine of time': Time and Love in Sidney's *Astrophel and Stella*", *Mosaic*, 13 (1979), 81–91.

Members of the Conference

Ashley C. Amos, *University of Toronto*
Margaret Anderson, *University of Toronto*
Heather A. R. Asals, *York University*
Elizabeth B. Bentley, *Toronto Board of Education*
G. E. Bentley, Jr., *University of Toronto*
William F. Blissett, *University of Toronto*
Ronald B. Bond, *University of Calgary*
Sharon Butler, *University of Toronto*
Mary J. Carnie, *Calgary*
Robert Hay Carnie, *University of Calgary*
Douglas D. C. Chambers, *University of Toronto*
Gordon Coggins, *Brock University*
Brian Corman, *University of Toronto*
J. A. Dainard, *University of Toronto*
Michael E. Darling, *Vanier College, St. Laurent*
A. H. de Quehen, *University of Toronto*

Micao Dean, *Carleton University*
Eric Domville, *University of Toronto*
Roman Dubinski, *University of Waterloo*
Robert D. Dunn, *Université Laval*
Alvin I. Dust, *University of Waterloo*
Saad M. El-Gabalawy, *University of Calgary*
W. Craig Ferguson, *Queen's University*
Denton Fox, *University of Toronto*
William Frost, *University of California, Santa Barbara*
Hilda Gifford, *Carleton University*
James Gray, *Dalhousie University*
Bert S. Hall, *University of Toronto*
Francess Halpenny, *University of Toronto*
A. C. Hamilton, *Queen's University*
W. H. Herendeen, *University of Toronto*
Evelyn J. Hinz, *University of Manitoba*
Heather J. Jackson, *University of Toronto*
J. R. de J. Jackson, *University of Toronto*
Henry D. Janzen, *University of Windsor*
Rina Kampeas, *York University*
Judith M. Kennedy, *St. Thomas University, Fredericton*
Richard F. Kennedy, *St. Thomas University, Fredericton*
Richard Landon, *University of Toronto*
David Latham, *University of Toronto*
Douglas LePan, *University of Toronto*
Trevor H. Levere, *University of Toronto*
Roger C. Lewis, *Acadia University*
Hugh R. MacCallum, *University of Toronto*
Charlotte W. Mangold, *Pennsylvania State University*
Lindsay A. Mann, *Carleton University*
James Means, *Université Laval*
R. Gordon Moyles, *University of Alberta*
Desmond Neill, *University of Toronto*
Peter D. Omnet, *University of Toronto*
John D. Peter, *University of Victoria*

Helen R. K. Peters, *University of Ottawa*
Allan Pritchard, *University of Toronto*
Mark Roberts, *University of Keele*
Bruce Ross, *Buffalo State College*
G. B. Shand, *York University*
W. James Shearer, *Woburn Collegiate Institute*
C. Anderson Silber, *University of Toronto*
Patricia E. Stone, *North York Public Library*
Claud A. Thompson, *University of Saskatchewan*
Prudence Tracy, *University of Toronto Press*
Germaine Warkentin, *University of Toronto*
Judith Williams, *University of Toronto Press*
Ian Willison, *British Library, Reference Division*
Milton Wilson, *University of Toronto*
James Woodruff, *University of Western Ontario*
George J. Zytaruk, *Nipissing University College*

Index